WRITERS AND THEIR WORK

ISOBEL ARMSTRONG
Consultant Editor

I0681845

JOHN BUNYAN

JOHN BUNYAN

Tamsin Spargo

NORTHCOTE
BRITISH
COUNCIL

© 2015 by Tamsin Spargo

First published in 2015 by Northcote House Publishers Ltd, Mary Tavy,
Tavistock, Devon, PL19 9PY, United Kingdom.
Tel: +44 (0) 1822 810066 Fax: +44 (0) 1822 810034.

British Library Cataloguing-in-Publication Data
A catalogue record for this book is available from the British Library

ISBN 978-0-7463-1049-6 hardcover
ISBN 978-0-7463-0982-7 paperback

Typeset by PDQ Typesetting, Newcastle-under-Lyme

This study is dedicated with thanks, for their example and support, to the scholars of the International John Bunyan Society.

Contents

Biographical and Historical Outline   ix

Abbreviations   xiii

1   Introduction   1

2   Bunyan's World   5

3   Bunyan as Preacher: Early Writing and
    Grace Abounding to the Chief of Sinners   15

4   Bunyan as Writer: *The Pilgrim's Progress*   30

5   *The Life and Death of Mr Badman*   47

6   *The Holy War*   54

7   *The Pilgrim's Progress: The Second Part*   61

8   *A Book for Boys and Girls*   72

9   Bunyan in the World   79

Notes   90

Select Bibliography   95

Index   102

Biographical and Historical Outline

1628   John Bunyan is born. Baptized on 30 November, he is the eldest child of Thomas Bunyan (1603–1676), a 'braseyer or tinker', and his second wife Margaret Bentley (1603–44). They live in the parish of Elstow near Bedford.

1629–40   Charles I rules without calling Parliament.

1642   Civil War begins.

1644   Bunyan's mother dies in June, his sister Margaret dies in July, and his father marries his third wife. In November Bunyan joins the Parliamentary army at Newport Pagnell.

1647   Bunyan is demobilized.

1649   Charles I tried and executed. Bunyan's first marriage (wife's name unknown).

1650   Compulsory attendance of parish church is suspended. Bunyan's first daughter (of four children), Mary, is born blind.

1653–8   Protectorate of Oliver Cromwell.

1655   Bunyan accepted into Bedford Congregation and soon starts preaching. John Gifford dies and is succeeded as minister by John Burton.

1656   Bunyan publishes *Some Gospel-Truths Opened*, the result of his public dispute with the Quakers.

1657   Cromwell is offered the Crown but refuses. Second Protectorate established.

1658   Cromwell dies, succeeded by his son Richard. Bunyan's wife dies. He publishes *A Few Sighs from Hell or the Groans of a Damned Soul*.

1659   Richard Cromwell abdicates. Bunyan's second marriage (to Elizabeth) takes place. He publishes *The*

Doctrine of the Law and Grace Unfolded, his most substantial doctrinal treatise.

1660   Monarchy restored and Charles II crowned. Episcopal structure of Church of England revived. Regicides tried and executed. Bunyan is arrested for holding a conventicle; his wife, in shock, has a premature baby who dies. John Burton dies. The Bedford Church becomes Nonconformist and meets secretly until 1672.

1661   Venner Rising by Fifth Monarchists in London. Bunyan sentenced to three months' imprisonment in Bedford gaol. As Bunyan refuses to agree not to preach the sentence is repeatedly extended until 1672. Bunyan makes shoe laces to support his family and writes. *Profitable Meditations*, a poem, is published.

1662   The Clarendon Code enacted (legislation that targets Nonconformists). Charles II's Declaration of Indulgence is overruled by Parliament. Under the Act of Uniformity, clergy who will not conform to the rules of the re-established Church are ejected from livings. Bunyan publishes *I Will Pray with the Spirit*, his attack on the Book of Common Prayer.

1663   Bunyan publishes *Christian Behaviour*, a conduct manual and the poem *Prison Meditations*. Samuel Fenn and John Whiteman are elected as pastors of Bedford church.

1664   First Conventicle Act.

1665   Bunyan publishes *The Holy City*, a millenarian treatise.

1666   Bunyan publishes *Grace Abounding to the Chief of Sinners*. He is released for several months but after preaching again is re-imprisoned.

1671   Bunyan is thought to have started writing *The Pilgrim's Progress* while writing *The Heavenly Footman* (published posthumously).

1672   John Whiteman dies, Bunyan is elected pastor. He is released from prison in March. Applies for a licence to preach under the Declaration of Indulgence and builds reputation as a preacher in Bedford and London. Publishes *A Defense of the Doctrine of*

Justification by Faith, an attack on the work of the Anglican Edward Fowler.

1673   Declaration of Indulgence withdrawn and persecution resumes. Bunyan publishes *Differences in Judgment about Water-Baptism no Bar to Communion*.

1674   Bunyan publishes *Peaceable Principles and True*, a response to attacks by Baptist writers. Bunyan is rumoured to have seduced a local woman, Agnes Beaumont, and helped her to poison her father. Agnes Beaumont is cleared of murder.

1676   Bunyan's father dies. Bunyan imprisoned again in December.

1677   Bunyan released from prison in June.

1678   *The Pilgrim's Progress* published.

1679   Censorship lapses when the Licencing Act expires. Parliament passes the first of three 'Exclusion' Bills to prevent the succession of the Roman Catholic James, Duke of York.

1680   Bunyan publishes *The Life and Death of Mr Badman* and a new edition of *Grace Abounding*, with rebuttals of the rumours from 1674.

1681   Charles II rules until 1685 without calling Parliament. Persecution of Dissenters is intensified.

1682   *The Holy War* is published.

1683   Rye House Plot and execution of leading Whigs.

1684   Bunyan publishes *Seasonable Counsel, or Advice to Sufferers* and *The Pilgrim's Progress: The Second Part*.

1685   Charles II dies and is succeeded by James II. The Monmouth rising fails. Bunyan transfers his property to his wife to avoid possible confiscation during 'Tory Revenge' on Nonconformists for involvement in 'Exclusion' attempts.

1686   *A Book for Boys and Girls* is published.

1687   James II's First Declaration of Indulgence. Bunyan is offered a place in the Bedford administration but refuses.

1688   James II's Second Declaration of Indulgence fails to improve his position. He flees to France as William of Orange, husband of Charles II's daughter Mary, lands in England. Bunyan is caught in heavy rain when riding to London after visiting Reading to reconcile a father and son. He contracts a fever and dies two weeks later at the house of his friend John Strudwick on 31 August. He is buried in Bunhill Fields, Finsbury, on 3 September. *The Advocateship of Jesus Christ, The Jerusalem Sinner Saved, A Discourse of the Building of the House of God, The Water of Life,* and *Solomon's Temple Spiritualized* are published.

1689 William and Mary are crowned. An Act of Toleration is passed. *The Acceptable Sacrifice* and *Mr. Bunyan's Last Sermon* are published.

1692 The first volume of a proposed folio edition of Bunyan's works is published under the editorship of Charles Doe. The, hitherto-unpublished, works are *An Exposition on the Ten First Chapters of Genesis, Of Justification by an Imputed Righteousness, Paul's Departure and Crown, Of the Trinity and a Christian, Of the Law and a Christian, Israel's Hope Encouraged, The Desire of the Righteous Granted, The Saints Privilege and Profit, Christ a Complete Saviour, The Saints Knowledge of Christ's Love, Of the House of the Forest of Lebanon,* and *Of Antichrist, and his Ruine.*

Abbreviations

GA	*Grace Abounding to the Chief of Sinners*, eds. John Stachniewski with Anita Pacheco (Oxford, 1998)
HW	*The Holy War*, eds. R. Sharrock and J. F. Forrest (Oxford, 1980)
MB	*The Life and Death of Mr Badman*, eds. J. F. Forrest and R. Sharrock (Oxford, 1988)
PP	*The Pilgrim's Progress*, ed. W. R. Owens (Oxford, 2003)
PP II	*The Pilgrim's Progress: The Second Part*, ed. W. R. Owens (Oxford, 2003)
MW III	*The Miscellaneous Works of John Bunyan, Volume III*, ed. J. S. McGee (Oxford, 1986)
MW IV	*The Miscellaneous Works of John Bunyan, Volume IV*, ed. T. L. Underwood (Oxford, 1989)
MW VI	*The Miscellaneous Works of John Bunyan, Volume VI*: *Poems*, ed. G. Midgley (Oxford, 1989)

1

Introduction

Witness my name, if Anagram'd to thee,
The Letters make, *Nu hony in a B.*

What does the name John Bunyan mean to modern men and
women? When the author composed this anagram, in an
afterword to a book called *The Holy War*, he was so well-known
that his work, and fame, had already spread far beyond his
native England. The publication of his most famous text, *The
Pilgrim's Progress*, had already made him what we would call a
household name across Europe and North America; soon the
book would be found across every continent making it one of
the international best sellers of all time. In the verse 'Advertise-
ment to the Reader' that was included with the later text,
Bunyan is defending himself against claims by people who felt
that he had not been the author of *The Pilgrim's Progress*:
'Insinuating as if I would shine/In name and fame by the worth
of another, Like some made rich by robbing of their Brother'
(*HW* 251). He claims sole authorship of the earlier text and
denies that anyone else, apart from God, had any involvement:
'Manner and matter too was all mine own, /Nor was it unto any
mortal known,/'Till I had done it' (*HW* 251). Bunyan concludes
his case for the defence with his confident and playful anagram,
sealing the association between John Bunyan and *The Pilgrim's
Progress* that has lasted until today.

Now John Bunyan is a name with which many people might
be familiar, through its association with the title of *The Pilgrim's
Progress*. But there are signs that the name and title have had a
different history to the writing that links them. English speakers
might still refer to a topography from his allegory, wallowing in
a Slough of Despond, living in one of the many streets called

'Mount Pleasant'; the magazine *Vanity Fair* unwittingly recreates the market for shallow pleasures that masked a harsh, unjust world; television quiz shows regularly ask 'Who wrote *The Pilgrim's Progress*?' or 'Can you name the famous allegory by John Bunyan?'. But when asked if they have read the book, far fewer people would say yes now than would have been the case in the nineteenth or early-twentieth centuries. There are notable exceptions: Bunyan's writings have consistently been read and disseminated within evangelical Christian movements and there has been steady, and recently burgeoning, academic attention to his work. But through the twentieth century, in common with other explicitly religious writers, Bunyan appeared to be falling victim to what some Western sociologists considered to be the inevitable march towards secularism.[1]

In this context even Bunyan's best-known work, *The Pilgrim's Progress*, seemed to be deprived of some of its force and relevance, to be, whatever its undoubted literary merit, a relic from a phase humanity was leaving behind. Literary critics and historians who approached Bunyan not from a position of faith but of scholarship continued to explore the ways in which his writings were influenced by, and contributed to, one of the most dynamic and turbulent periods in British history. This study is informed by, and written from, this position, arguing that Bunyan's writings are important documents with significant histories of production, dissemination, and reception. But Bunyan's writings are explicitly Christian and cannot be productively explored if the religious faith that motivates them is not taken seriously; it does not have to be shared by the reader, but has to be acknowledged as a driving and determining force.

Towards the end of the twentieth century it would have been fair to say that a majority of Western scholars, and universities, would have judged the study of religious texts as a minority concern. But as the dramatic events of the early-twenty-first century have shown, the assumed march to a secular future was at best a partial vision and at worst an arrogant dream that ignored the millions of followers of various faiths across the world. While there are many other dimensions, socio-economic and political, to the conflicts that have dominated our new millennium, the role played by religion in shaping our lives has been brought dramatically into focus. As debates about fundamentalism – Islamic, Christian, and, some would argue, scientific/atheist – now engage scholars across disciplines and national boundaries, there is fresh impetus to explore the texts that derive from, and sustain, religious faith. In this context, as scholars in various disciplines explore the production of meaning from what some call a 'post-secular' stance and others a return to religion, Bunyan's works are attracting renewed attention.

In the writings of John Bunyan we encounter a Christian world view that might, although the term is of later origin and frequently used reductively, be called fundamentalist. This writer's faith is based on what has been called a 'literalist' interpretation of the Bible.[2] Those of us with less steadfast belief, or with none, may glimpse something of the difference between our understanding of our place in the world and those of a man defined fundamentally, by faith. But the encounter with Bunyan cannot be reduced even to the terms even by which he might have understood his life and work. Whenever we put pen to paper, or finger to keyboard, no matter how fervently we wish to convey a clear, particular message, we must accept that, inspired by God, driven by conviction, or simply hopeful of a positive reception, we are ultimately in the hands of our readers. Even a simple sentence can be understood, interpreted, differently both from the author's intended meaning and from other readers'. When writing is as rich in imagery and symbolism, as dense and varied in allusion, and as dramatic and memorable in narrative, as Bunyan's most ambitious works, it defies reductive reading.

The John Bunyan whose life and work will be introduced in this short study is certainly a man of his time and a man of strong, defining faith, but he was also an extraordinary and complex figure whose work challenges us as modern readers. He had no ambitions to be an author in our modern sense but wrote more than sixty texts. The vast majority were treatises and written sermons, extending or replacing an oral ministry that was Bunyan's true calling, but his writings also included one of the best sellers of all time (*The Pilgrim's Progress*), a spiritual autobiography of unrivalled intensity (*Grace Abounding to the Chief of Sinners*), a satire on sinfulness that revealed the dilemmas of nascent capitalism (*The Life and Death of Mr Badman*), a dramatic psychomachia of a war-torn age (*The Holy War*). It is hard to imagine many writers with a greater range, and even fewer who could produce such work while enduring the sufferings of poverty, imprisonment, and persecution, not to mention what we might call his 'day job' of ministering to an extensive church community.

This volume can only introduce and outline some of the main features of Bunyan's life and work. After a chapter on the historical, social, and cultural context in which John Bunyan wrote, it will focus in turn on each of his main narrative, or literary, works, as these were his explicitly experimental, or ambitious, texts. Each chapter will explore key themes and characteristics of the texts and consider, briefly, the social and theological factors that may have impacted on their production, Bunyan's other writing at the time, as well as key events in his life. The study will conclude by considering the afterlife of some of Bunyan's texts, especially *The Pilgrim's Progress*, that has both extended and diversified the author's influence across world and time.

2

Bunyan's World

It is a commonplace of contemporary literary criticism that looking into an author's life for the ultimate explanations of his or her writing is at worst a futile and at best a frustrating exercise because the meanings and effects of texts are created through the way that they are read and interpreted by diverse readers at different times. It would be a foolhardy critic, however, who suggested that one would make the most of reading the writings of John Bunyan without knowing something of his dramatic life and of the turbulent times in which his writings were composed and first published. Bunyan's life was inextricably bound up with the momentous political, social and religious changes of the seventeenth century and his writings responded to and intervened in the debates and arguments that accompanied and occasioned those changes.

Some readers may value his writings as a source of information about society in the period of their composition, while others look to knowledge about the period to illuminate aspects of Bunyan's writings that are unclear today, yet others, of whom I count myself one, are fascinated by the dialectic process we may see at work between text and context.

There is another vital dimension to Bunyan's world that this chapter will explore, which is for some readers the greatest challenge in appreciating his writing and for others its greatest gift. Bunyan was, without doubt, a man of his time but he was also, and profoundly, a writer working in the service of a particular religious understanding of the place of human beings in the world. While many of the details of Bunyan's beliefs, his approach to living in their light, and of communicating them to others, will be explored in the sections of this study that focus on individual texts, this chapter will offer an introduction to the particular strand of Protestant theology that informed his writings and defined his life.

SOCIAL AND POLITICAL CONTEXT

John Bunyan lived through some of the most tumultuous days of English and British history when the world was, in the scriptural phrase that took on particular resonance in the period, 'turned upside down' (Acts 17.6). He was born in 1628, the year in which Parliament passed the Petition of Right and placed the first limits on the power of the king, only to be ignored as Charles I sought to establish an increasingly absolutist monarchy. He died in 1688, just two months before the Glorious Revolution in which the Protestant settlement was saved by William of Orange's victory over the Catholic James II. Between these years England had been, in turns, a battleground in a civil war between its absolutist monarch and its Parliament, a revolutionary society in which the king was tried for treason and executed and a republic proclaimed, and a kingdom once again. Although Bunyan's direct engagement with politics, understood in modern terms, was limited, his religious practices, as preacher, minister and writer, involved him directly in the battles and debates of his age and brought him into conflict with those whose authority he challenged.

Bunyan was born and raised in Elstow, a village just south of Bedford, a town in the eastern midlands. He was the eldest of three children of Thomas Bunyan and his second wife Mary Bentley. His exact birth date is not recorded but he was baptized, according to parish church records of 30 November. Bunyan's family was poor and although the Bunyans had held a more socially 'respectable' position in the sixteenth century, with a smallholding, a tract of land enough to raise food for the family, Thomas Bunyan was a brazier or tinker as his son would be. In *Grace Abounding to the Chief of Sinners*, Bunyan claimed that his father's family was 'of that rank that is meanest, and most despised of all the families in the Land' (*GA* 6) and it is clear, from his own writings and other records, that his trade was indeed looked down on.

This social and economic decline in the family's fortunes has been linked to wider changes in English society, as many smallholders were adversely affected by the consolidation of the great estates that took place through the sixteenth century; it has also been seen as an influence on Bunyan's views of social and spiritual exclusion.[1] Certainly Bunyan's upbringing was anything but privileged. He was, however, sent to school, which was by no means customary for the children of the lower artisan class. His father does not appear to have been able to write but the young John was sent to school 'to learn both to read and write' (*GA* 6). In his own words he succeeded in both 'according to the rate of other poor men's children, though to my shame I confess, I did soon loose that little I learnt, and that even almost utterly' (*GA* 6). Throughout his life, Bunyan would emphasize his lack of conventional learning, often as a way of foregrounding the greater value and significance of individual reading of Scripture and communion with God, but, while his writings reveal that he was better read than he claimed, it is entirely credible that his formal education had little immediate impact beyond the all-important introduction to literacy.

Bunyan left school early to work in his father's trade. There are few records of his childhood but, as the next chapter will show, the adult Bunyan's comments on his childhood suggest he was not only fond of the traditional sports and pastimes of village life but also, if not the greatest of sinners, then prone to swearing, lying and blasphemy as well as acute anxiety about his sins. He sounds, in short, like a regular village lad. Bunyan makes few comments about his parents, although he does voice his regret that his father did not teach him to speak without swearing. In the summer of 1644, when he was fifteen or sixteen, Bunyan's mother and younger sister both died. By November that year he was serving in the Parliamentary army while his father swiftly remarried, as was the custom at the time.

The Civil War had started in 1642 but it was the culmination of tensions between the reigning monarch, Charles I, and Parliament, that had been building for decades. The political, economic, social, and religious dimensions of the conflict are too many and complex to be expounded here, but a summary to fit a nutshell might say that Charles was asserting the autocratic rights of a divinely-ordained monarch to rule according to his views and priorities, while Parliament demanded that the monarch recognize the rights and processes enshrined in law. Charles had dissolved Parliament and ruled in person from 1629 to 1640, bypassing Parliament to impose changes that proved intolerable to many across the social spectrum.

While some, including a number of the aristocracy and landed gentry, objected particularly to the erosion of traditional rights, others were appalled by the introduction of changes to the ceremonies and practices of the Church of England that they believed heralded a return to Roman Catholicism and saw as a betrayal of the Protestant reformation. By 1638, Charles had found himself at war with the Scots, who vehemently opposed the imposition of a revised Book of Common Prayer and the increased authority of the bishops, and, having failed to levy money independently through a Ship Tax that was effectively money demanded without parliamentary authority, was forced to recall Parliament.

In 1640 Parliament reined in the powers of the monarch and established itself as part of the constitution by making it impossible for the monarch to dissolve it. As social unrest raged at home, caused by opposition to Charles's economic and religious impositions, and the Catholic Irish rose against English rule, passions on both sides intensified. Parliamentary radicals were determined to protect and extend their political gains and protect the protestant settlement, while some who had opposed the king's autocratic approach were now driven to his cause by fear of social breakdown. Eventually both sides drew up their armies and England was plunged into civil war.

Bunyan joined the army, at some point in 1644, when war had been waged across the country for two years with neither side gaining a decisive advantage. The name John Bunnion or John Bunian appears in the Parliamentary army's muster rolls, but we do not know if Bunyan volunteered, for political or economic reasons, or was conscripted. The meagreness of the historical record, and of Bunyan's own comments on this subject, has even led to conjecture that he might have served in the Royalist forces, but most scholars agree that he served in the Parliamentary army.[2] Whatever Bunyan's own motives for serving, life in the army must have had an impact on the young man. Bunyan was based in a garrison in Newport Pagnell in Buckinghamshire and while we do not know much about his time as a soldier, his writing, such as *The Holy War*, is informed by military experience. It is also likely, although not incontrovertible, that the young Bunyan had been influenced by the religious, and political, radicalism of the army. By the time he left the army at the age of nineteen, when his regiment was demobilized in 1647, the Parliamentary troops had been transformed into a highly disciplined fighting force, known as the New Model Army, which would eventually defeat the Royalist enemy.

The New Model Army attempted to turn ordinary men and boys into well-disciplined soldiers, but it also functioned as a debating arena in which radical political ideas and groups flourished. In the army and also more widely, as state censorship of pamphlets and books broke down in wartime, radical ideas circulated on an unprecedented scale. Before and after the defeat of the king, groups like the Levellers openly discussed the nature of the political, economic and social order and envisioned a revolutionary society, a 'world turned upside down', while other groups, like Baptists, called for a radical revision of religious life, far removed from the approach of the Established Church.[3] Some, known as 'millenarians' believed that Scriptural interpretation indicated that the war was one of the signs that the end of the world, and the second coming of Jesus to start the reign of God on earth, was imminent. Millenarianism, which Bunyan espouses in his writings, was not an unusual belief in the period, but some groups such as Fifth Monarchists, felt it their duty to hasten the return, prompting fears among those in positions of authority, local and national, that these soldiers for Christ might keep fighting.

Bunyan was discharged from the army when his regiment was demobilized in 1647 and returned to his home village to take up his trade as a tinker. In 1649 Charles I was captured, tried, and executed for treason, the monarchy abolished, and a republic known as the Commonwealth was declared. The political and religious radicals of the New Model Army were influential in the early stages of this new society, and the world that had been turned upside down in the civil war seemed set on a course of continuing change. Change there certainly was, but the exigencies of maintaining social order and the conflicting interests of the various social groups who had united against Charles I, meant that the liberties of the 1640s would be curtailed. By 1652 the radical groups had been marginalized and in 1653 Oliver Cromwell was invited to take up a new role as Lord Protector. It would be a misrepresentation to say that the 1650s saw an inexorable move back to a more hierarchical society; there had been significant changes to the social and religious order. Yet, although Oliver Cromwell refused the crown when it was offered to him in 1657, when he died a year later he was succeeded as Lord Protector by his son Richard. It is not hard to imagine the reactions of some of the radicals, but by now the regime was financially crippled, internally riven by conflict between factions and within a year Richard had been forced to stand down and the republic was brought to an end with an invitation from the dominant parliamentary group, to another son to succeed his father. On 8 May 1660 Parliament declared that Charles II had been lawful monarch since the date of his father's execution.

The Commonwealth and Protectorate were effectively excised from the official record, but the changes made in those decades and the impact on people's ways of viewing their society and their place in it would endure.

RELIGION

Shortly after leaving the army, Bunyan married a young woman whose name we do not know but who brought with her a dowry that would make a real difference to her husband. The dowry was not money but two popular Puritan books: Lewis Bayly's *Practice of Piety* and Arthur Dent's *The Plaine Mans Pathway to Heaven*. The significance that Bunyan allots to this dowry marks his move from outward conforming to established religion to committing himself to a different understanding of faith.

When Bunyan was born, all English adults were expected to attend their local Church of England and could be fined for failing to do so, on top of the tithe, or tenth, of one's income that was to be paid as a matter of course. Since the break with the Roman Catholic Church in the reign of Henry VIII, church and state hierarchies had been bound together and subjects were expected to demonstrate their loyalty and obedience to both: the

Acts of Supremacy (1534 and 1559) made the monarch first Supreme Head and then Supreme Governor of the Church of England, presiding over a church with an episcopalian structure (a hierarchy of archbishops, bishops and lower orders of ordained ministers reporting to them); the Act of Uniformity (1559) made the Book of Common Prayer, and its associated orders of service, including prayers for the monarch, compulsory. The Protestant reform movement that swept across parts of Europe through the early-modern period led large numbers of Christians to question, and challenge, this traditional, conservative understanding of the place and duties of the church and of the believer. By the seventeenth century, religious radicals from the Puritan tradition were at the heart of the revolution that violently removed the royal head from the body of the Church of England.

In the Commonwealth and Protectorate period, the Church of England was not disestablished, but bishops were abolished and the Act of Uniformity repealed. Everyone was still obliged to pay tithes but less radical independent churches and groups were tolerated to a certain extent. It has passed into folklore that the Commonwealth abolished Christmas as well as maypoles, and while there are exaggerated readings of Puritan joylessness, there was certainly a systematic stripping away of the ceremonials and feast-days and practices that linked the church to its older, Catholic and pre-Christian roots. But although people like Bunyan still enjoyed their traditional sports and games, albeit guiltily in his case, Bedfordshire was an area where there was great sympathy for the Puritan way.

In this period, Bunyan, working hard as a tinker to support a growing family including his first-born daughter, Mary, who was blind, was beset by anxiety about his spiritual condition as he had been since childhood. As he recalled in *Grace Abounding to the Chief of Sinners*, as a young man he veered between indulging in games and worse and agonizing about his apparently slim chance of salvation. After returning from the army, he regularly attended his village church, sometimes more than once each Sunday, admiring the 'High-place, Priest, Clerk, Vestments, Service, and what else' (*GA* 9). This would have been the remodelled Church of England, but Bunyan still felt that what he later called 'superstition' (*GA* 9) was merely finding

11

comfort by conforming to external rituals. His life was then transformed in the nearby town of Bedford, when he was encouraged by an encounter with some female believers to become part of a congregation who worshipped under the guidance of the minister John Gifford.

This was a newly formed church that has been identified as Baptist, shortened from 'anabaptist', signalling a congregation of believers who were baptised as *adults* when they had made a full commitment to Christian belief rather than as babies or children as a matter of convention. It is difficult to apply labels to churches in the period, especially as names for denominations have since come to mean different things, and many critics prefer to define Bunyan's chosen church as Congregationalist. Whatever its denomination, here Bunyan found a fellowship that would sustain him, and, in due course, a pastoral and creative role that would define his life. In 1655 he and his family moved to Bedford and while he still worked as a tinker, his true vocation would be found through this church. The church, and Bunyan, would experience the dramatic, and often traumatic, consequences of political change in the decades to follow but external pressures, even violent persecution, could never matter to someone of Bunyan's religious persuasion, and temperament, as much as the inner struggle for salvation. The remainder of this chapter will explore some of the tenets of the faith that Bunyan shared with the Bedford congregation and how they shaped his life and writing.

Bunyan's work must be read as part of the tradition that was initiated by Puritan reformers who stressed the relationship between individual Christians and God, through Christ and Scripture, rather than through the intermediaries of priest or ritual. This is not the place to explore the complexities of the theological positions that emerged and developed from the early-modern period to the late-seventeenth century, but anyone who wishes to understand the force of Bunyan's writing in his own age must acknowledge the impact of two related theological concepts that structured his belief and thought. These concepts – predestination and justification by faith alone – derived from the work of John Calvin, the radical protestant theologian from Geneva, whose modifications to earlier protestant thought are known as Calvinism and whose ideas were extremely influential among radical Christian groups in the mid-seventeenth century. Although Bunyan makes no reference to Calvin in his writings, in contrast to the weight he assigns in *Grace Abounding to the Chief of Sinners* to the thought and example of the other great Reformation figure, Martin Luther, it is Calvinism that implicitly provides a dynamic, and possibly traumatic, impetus for much religious, and creative, work in the period including his own.

The type of Calvinism that was most influential in England argued that an individual's ultimate salvation or damnation was preordained by God before his or her creation. This theory of predestination divided people into two groups: those who were elect (the saved) and those who were reprobate (the damned), and insisted that the individual could do nothing to change this assignment. This connected with another key idea: salvation through faith alone. According to this view, the penances and indulgences of Roman Catholicism were worthless and the good works encouraged by the Church of England could not undo God's decision. If this belief potentially threatened the idea of established order in state or church, it could also be distressing for believers. It might reassure a poor man that a rich man could not 'buy' spiritual advantage, but, if everything was pre-ordained how would an anxious Christian know if he or she was saved or damned? If a human being is powerless to change this divinely-ordained destiny, is there any cause for hope or for trying to live a Christian life as laid down in Scripture?

Some groups followed the theory of predestination to a logical conclusion and argued that if an individual's salvation or damnation was already decided then his or her behaviour need not be bound by conventional morality. The most notorious group who espoused this idea, antinomianism, were known as Ranters who flourished in the revolutionary period, and while we have no evidence of Bunyan encountering Levellers or political radicals, he explicitly mentions this group and their appeal in *Grace Abounding to the Chief of Sinners*. But Bunyan became part of a different congregation, committed to the model of Calvinist double-predestination but trying to live godly lives in a fallen world.

Bunyan's Calvinist Christianity was not an easy creed. If Calvinist double-predestination could be taken as grounds for

13

crippling depression or for amoral excess, it also proved, as the rest of this book will explore, to be the catalyst for some of the most striking cultural production in the English language including Bunyan's prolific and varied writing.

3

Bunyan as Preacher: Early Writing and *Grace Abounding to the Chief of Sinners*

On 12 November 1660 John Bunyan was standing, Bible in hand, in a barn in the village of Lower Samsell. He was praying with the local people and preparing to preach to them when a constable entered and arrested him. Bunyan was called before the Bedfordshire magistrates and questioned about his activities. After a preliminary hearing he waited in gaol for seven weeks before being tried at the quarter-sessions. The indictment was, in Bunyan's words, 'That John Bunyan of the town of Bedford, labourer, being a person of such and such conditions, he hath (since such a time) devilishly and perniciously abstained from coming to church to hear divine service, and is a common upholder of several unlawful meetings and conventicles, to the great disturbance and distraction of the good subjects of this kingdom, contrary to the laws of our sovereign lord the king, &c'.[1]

The king was Charles II, recently restored to his father's throne, initiating a period when traditional hierarchies were reintroduced, old scores were settled, and religious dissent, in person or in print, rigorously policed. While the coming decades would see brief episodes of strategic reduction in the persecution of religious Nonconformists, this was a dangerous time to follow the dictates of conscience rather than the law. Bunyan was charged under the Elizabethan *Act for Retaining the Queen's Subjects in their Due Obedience* of 1593. This law was originally a response to separatist Puritan churches and was used again in 1660 to enforce religious conformity. From the wording of the indictment it might only have been Bunyan's attendance at the wrong sort of religious meetings that was the problem. But as accounts of his trial show, Bunyan was a more troublesome, even threatening, figure, an unlicensed preacher, and this was the true reason for his arrest and prosecution. After formally joining the Bedford church in 1655, the year when John Gifford died and was succeeded by John Burton, Bunyan swiftly became active, not only as a member of the congregation but as what we would today call a 'lay', or unordained, preacher. To be admitted to the type of church that Bunyan joined required making a formal profession of faith, today often known as either a 'spiritual autobiography' or a 'conversion narrative'. In Bunyan's case this would form the basis of *Grace Abounding to the Chief of Sinners*, the earliest of his writings to have earned lasting acclaim, and which will be considered later in this chapter. As his own conversion narrative showed, Bunyan found that he was called not only to faith but to try to reach others, to preach and being called to preach brought him into direct confrontation with the authorities.

Bunyan could apparently have avoided arrest as he was warned about the arrest warrant before he went to Lower Samsell. The consequences of arrest would be severe: if prosecuted Bunyan might face punishment that was unlikely to include death, although he did fear that might be the case, but would almost inevitably mean loss of liberty and separation from his family. Bunyan's first wife had died in 1658, leaving four children; Bunyan had married a second wife, Elizabeth, in 1659. He chose to risk the consequences because, as he reassured a friend, 'our cause is good, we need not be ashamed of it, to preach Gods word, it is so good a work, that we shall be well rewarded, if we suffer for that', and because he was anxious not to be a poor example to those who had come to hear him (*GA* 98).

By 1660 Bunyan had acquired something of a reputation as a preacher in the Bedford area. His years within the congregation led by John Gifford and later John Burton had helped him to find his own calling and although he was not a minister in the Bedford church he had found a voice of some authority. In the judgment of the local political authorities, however, his calling was to be a tinker and his voice was to be silenced.

To the justices who tried him John Bunyan had no authority to preach. In 'A Relation of the Imprisonment of Mr John Bunyan', a collection of documents written by Bunyan, but not published until long after his death, Bunyan recorded his own exchanges with the judges and those of his wife. In it he recalled being advised by one judge that 'if I would but leave off preaching, and follow my calling, I should have the justice's favour, and be acquitted presently' (*GA* 103). But he was not intimidated by the judges' scorn for his social status and refusal to recognize that he was bound by his duty to obey a greater authority than any worldly court of law. The disruptive power of the sects lay not in encouraging individuals to disobey an unjust or persecuting ruler, but rather in insisting that ruler, judge and tinker alike are all required to act in obedience to an absolute authority, whose true meaning is inscribed not in any constitution or law of man but in the living Word, the Scriptures as the visible and audible transcription of the ever, and everywhere, present deity.

Throughout the trial Bunyan contended with the judges, challenging their authority by grounding his defence in his knowledge of Scripture. When attacked for refusing to conform to the practice of using the *Book of Common Prayer*, he turned to the one Book that matters: 'I said, shew me the place in the epistles, where the Common Prayer-book is written, or one text of Scripture, that commands me to read it, and I will use it. But yet, notwithstanding, said I, they that have a mind to use it, they have their liberty; that is, I would not keep them from it, but for our parts, we can pray to God without it' (*GA* 108–9). Similarly, when a judge 'asked me where I had my authority?' to preach, Bunyan cited Scriptural exhortations to those who have received 'the gift' to exercise it, to 'speak as the oracles of God' (*GA* 109–10). By the end of the trial it was clear that the two sides had reached an impasse. Bunyan was establishing a position we might today call passive resistance, arguing: 'Sir, said I, the law hath provided me two ways of obeying: The one to do that which I in my conscience do believe that I am bound to do, actively; and where I cannot obey actively, there I am willing to lie down, and to suffer what they shall do unto me' (*GA* 116).

Bunyan was found guilty and sent to prison with a threat of banishment or death hanging over him if he failed to abandon his commitment to preaching. Although spared the severest punishments, his continued refusal to promise to stop preaching meant that Bunyan spent the next twelve years in Bedford gaol. In the early days a relatively lenient regime allowed him to make some brief visits to London and elsewhere, allowing him to maintain some pastoral contacts, but this was a harsh life. Prisons were unhealthy as well as uncomfortable and his enforced separation from his wife and children, including his blind daughter Mary, was painful. His wife Elizabeth had argued forcefully on his behalf with the justices, implicitly challenging Bunyan's own adherence to St Paul's prohibition on women speaking in public; she also gave birth to a premature baby who died. It is hard to imagine a family enduring greater hardship.[2] Bunyan's prison labour, making boot laces, can have been of limited assistance to them and separation from members of his church, and those to whom he was accustomed to preaching, was just as difficult. If the authorities had hoped to silence this awkward tinker, however, they had badly miscalculated. By imprisoning a preacher they helped to make a writer.

Prevented from addressing his congregation in person, Bunyan turned to writing instead. In doing so he began to reach a wider and greater audience than he could ever have spoken to directly, escaping not only the temporary constraints imposed on him by his persecutors, but also those of time and place. Writing brought challenges as well as opportunities for a man driven by the need to attend not only to his own spiritual condition but to those of others. In an age of intermittently punitive regulation of the press, there were legal hazards but the world of Nonconformist and supportive publishers offered encouragement and fellowship in communicating God's message as well as disseminating Bunyan's writings.[3] Reaching an ever-wider readership confounded the attempts of the authorities to prevent him from addressing them in person and could overcome the barriers of space and time, but a preacher in print cannot read his congregation or even know if those reading are committed to God. An author cannot assess whether or not a point had been successfully made, whether a reader understands his words as he intends. As Bunyan embarks on the writing side of his mission, we can hear the robust, lively voice of the popular preacher and we can see his increasing

18

confidence in experimenting with the formal and literary possibilities of writing. Bunyan learns to entertain as well as educate, to adapt worldly techniques for God's purposes. But we can also see his anxiety about the possibility of misinterpreting, his growing awareness that a reader might be entertained instead of attending to the message. Later chapters of this study explore this concern as it frames some of Bunyan's most ambitious texts but for now it is enough to note this productive tension at the heart of Bunyan's writing.

FIRST WRITINGS

Bunyan had written before his imprisonment and his earliest writings reveal much about his pastoral involvement, and preaching style, as well as his theological position. This is not the place for an exhaustive survey of all of Bunyan's early publications but it is worth considering two in particular, as they reveal his priorities at the time, both doctrinally and pastorally, which would inform much of his work. They also typify two strands of Bunyan's writing: the combative and the expository, although these are generally intertwined within an over-arching aim to edify, to help the reader to understand and appreciate God's grace.

His first text, *Some Gospel-Truths Opened*, was published in 1656, a year after his baptism and acceptance into the congregation of the Bedford Church. The treatise was a polemic addressed to Quakers with whom Bunyan was engaged in a heated dispute. The Quakers, whose radical beliefs and disruptive social practices bore little relation to our modern stereotype of quiet pacifism, had become quite influential in the Bedford area at this time. They might have been seen as rivals in the battle for souls, but the clash of Quakers and Baptists was more than a territorial skirmish. The Quakers also argued for a version of Christianity that was anathema to traditional Calvinists like Bunyan, stressing the 'divine light within' each human being and holding highly unorthodox views of Christ and the role of free will. While their views may be appealing to our individualistic, twenty-first-century society, to Bunyan they were dangerously akin to those of the Ranters, a radical group that had attracted him in his youth. At the core of Ranter belief, and the reason for their alleged amoral excesses, was antinomianism, the extreme interpretation of the consequences of predestination that held that the elect had no need to obey social or moral law. By the time he had found his calling as a preacher and writer, he was convinced that not only Ranterism but Quakerism were un-Christian.

The treatise combines personal, experiential detail and a direct combative style. Sometimes savage, abusive, and even amusing, in his representation of Quakers, Bunyan poses questions to the reader and repeats key phrases just as a preacher would. There are also signs of the lively style in which recognizable features from the reader's own everyday world are used to bring home the argument. He claims, for example, that the Quakers are expounding the very same opinions as the Ranters, except 'the Ranters had made them thred-bare at an Ale-House, and the Quakers have set a new glosse upon them again, by an outward legall holinesse, or righteousnesse' (MW I 139).[4] The aim is clearly to convince, using all the rhetorical skills at his disposal and in God's service. Bunyan is using writing as an extension of a pastoral duty to point out the dangerous errors of Quaker doctrine as well as attacking his rivals. One reason for the vehemence of his denunciation of the Quakers was his own doctrinal position, which clearly stressed the role of grace over that of the law and might have left him open to similar charges of antinomianism.

Bunyan's need to distance himself from Christians associated with antinomianism was, in part, because of the position he outlines in another early treatise. *The Doctrine of the Law and Grace Unfolded* (1659) is an exposition of Bunyan's understanding of the twin covenants of Christianity. God's first covenant with humankind is the Covenant of the Law, also known as the Covenant of Works, signalled by the Ten Commandments delivered to Moses on Mount Sinai, which establish the rules for godly conduct. This stringent covenant that marks for damnation anyone who sins, or breaks these commandments, dominates the Old Testament and fuels the guilt and anxiety that plagued Bunyan, and his fellow believers, but also urged them to seek redemption and forgiveness. That redemption and forgiveness of sins, leading to the possibility of salvation, is afforded by the second covenant, the Covenant of Grace; this covenant, outlined in St Paul's Letter to the Corinthians, succeeds and supervenes that of the Law, offering salvation, by God's Grace, through his Son, Jesus Christ's sacrifice in propitiation for human sin. The theological position Bunyan establishes in this treatise is, as critics have recognized, one that could be seen to define his individual understanding of the relationship between God and humanity and to underpin his writings and approach to writing.[5] The treatise establishes Bunyan's firm commitment to the principal of justification by faith alone, his recognition of the inadequacy and perils of stressing formal or ritual aspects of religion, positions which might seem to ally him with the more extreme, antinomian groups. But Bunyan believes in the force of both covenants and here shares the comforts of the Covenant of Grace with those who, like him, had trembled with proper fear under the Covenant of the Law. The treatise combines meticulous, lengthy exposition of all the pertinent Scriptural references, with an accessible and dramatic prose style and a direct address to the reader that shows the text's roots in oral address. While listening to Bunyan preach may not have been a comfortable experience, it must have been memorable.

Bunyan continued to write the treatises that served as virtual sermons or disputes throughout his time in prison and, indeed, throughout his life. The subjects cover conventional theological matters but also touch on matters that arose within the Bedford congregation and in a wider social context. Two years after his argument with his judges about the *Book of Common Prayer*, in 1662, when a new Act of Uniformity prescribed its use in all churches, and required that all ministers be ordained by bishops, he roundly denounced it in an anonymous treatise *I Will Pray with the Spirit*. Together with other laws enacted at the time, which banned conventicles or worship groups of five or more, and barred those who did not take Anglican communion from public office and even from taking degrees at Oxford and Cambridge Universities, the legislation is known as the Clarendon Code, after the Lord Chancellor, Edward Hyde, Earl of Clarendon. The Acts were designed to exclude those who would not conform from positions of influence or from forming independent churches and remained on the statute books and were partially enforced until the nineteenth century. While the consequences were harsh, and, combined with censorship, made life difficult for the targets of the legislation, the Clarendon Code and its enforcers also helped to produce an identity for those who it sought to exclude: Baptists, Quakers, and other groups became known as 'Nonconformists', a term hitherto applied to those within the Church of England who would not conform to official rituals and dress. While the label itself means more to those studying them than it will have to the seventeenth-century Nonconformists, the experience of persecution heightened a desire to help and support one another, in person and through writing, and so contributed to the development of a rich and enduring Nonconformist culture.

Bunyan's writing allowed him to maintain a sense of pastoral connection with the Bedford congregation, offering spiritual guidance and attacking unacceptable doctrinal or political positions and laws. He also, as a consequence of the persecution of Nonconformists, had a new audience within the gaol, as he found himself sharing his quarters with others who had been arrested for refusing to comply with the law. This group of prisoners, communicating with their congregations outside, effectively became a hub for Nonconformist activity in the area, confounding the attempt to silence and isolate them. To this group of informed and passionate believers Bunyan preached sermons that were then published, such as *The Holy City* (1665).

He also experimented with different types of writing that some have argued may have been designed to supplement his meagre earnings making laces. He wrote some poems on religious themes, starting with *Profitable Meditations* (1661) and then *Prison Meditations* (1663) that explicitly alluded to his captive status. The latter poem was first published with *Christian Behaviour*, which adapted the popular form of a conduct book, offering advice on how the Christian should behave within the household. This manual 'Teaching Husbands, Wives, Parents, Children, Masters, Servants, &c. how to walk so as to please God,' can be seen, like his disputes with the Quakers, as establishing clear distance between Bunyan and the antinomians who took divine grace as a licence for immorality.[6]

However, Bunyan was passionate in his conviction that merely behaving outwardly in ways that seemed to adhere to the precepts of Christianity, whether by attending services, mouthing prayers, or even adopting what we might think of as good moral standards in dealings with others, was of no value without fully accepting that salvation, granted by God's grace, could come through faith in Jesus Christ. Yet sin was sin, with all its consequences set out in Scripture, so the Christian was duty bound to behave well. It is possible, if somewhat reductive, to think of this as Bunyan finding a middle way between the stress on outward ritual and ceremony in the Church of England and the rejection of the law and morality in the various antinomian groups.

This way, however, had neither been easy to reach nor would it be easy to travel, as the text published in 1666 that, for many readers, established Bunyan as a great writer as well as a passionate Christian, dramatized with striking effect.

GRACE ABOUNDING TO THE CHIEF OF SINNERS

> Children, Grace be with you, Amen. I being taken from you in presence, and so tied up, that I cannot perform that duty that from God doth lie upon me, to you-ward, for your further edifying and building up in Faith and Holiness, &c., yet that you may see my Soul hath fatherly care and desire after your spiritual and everlasting welfare; I now once again, as before from the top of Shenir and Hermon, so now from the Lions Dens, and from the Mountains of the Leopards (Song 4. 8), do look yet after you all, greatly longing to see your safe arrival into THE desired haven. (GA 3)

These words opened Bunyan's letter accompanying the published text of *Grace Abounding to the Chief of Sinners*, dedicating it to the congregation from whom he was forcibly separated. Bunyan was not yet the official minister of the Bedford congregation, which would happen, through election in 1672, but he had already, the text suggests, taken up a position of some responsibility towards his fellow members even in prison: Bunyan, as 'father', acknowledges a '*duty that from God doth lie upon me*' to guide his 'children' into 'THE *desired haven*'. The figure of the father is accompanied by a number of scriptural quotations and references in the first person that were originally attributed to Solomon, Paul and Samson. Bunyan is also linked by analogy with Moses and with the greatest of human shepherds within the Christian narrative, David. Together these allusions create a figure of some authority within a community of people who understand each other. It is important to remember this when we turn to the body of the text.

The Bunyan depicted in the body of the text is, for the most part, a man with little authority or certainty. *Grace Abounding to the Chief of Sinners* relates Bunyan's experience of the process of conversion from his spiritually carefree youth, to his first awareness of sin and consequent struggles to accept the imputed righteousness of Christ. It is a dramatic and intense narrative, effectively recreating the psychological traumas of the younger man as he experiences the depths of despair as well as moments of reassurance. As a record of the traumatic and dramatic effect of profound anxiety, this text makes vivid the yearning and terror that fear about one's spiritual condition could induce in a young man from a village in Bedfordshire. Yet this is not only an exploration of one man's agonizing search. It is, to be sure, a testament and a testimony, enabling the older Bunyan to re-present his experiences, but it is also a text designed to have a practical impact. *Grace Abounding* takes its reader through an educative process of witnessing, and ideally learning from, Bunyan's trials and errors as he learns to truly understand and accept the role of divine grace in his search for salvation.

The text is generally categorized in criticism as a spiritual autobiography, but the modern reader who approaches *Grace Abounding* expecting to find the self-revelations and confessions of a secular autobiography will be disappointed. Bunyan includes very few details of his family life or material circumstances unless they serve to make a point about his spiritual condition. Yet as we study this text we may learn something about the nature of autobiography and biography more generally. For although Bunyan stresses that he is telling 'the thing as it was' (*GA* 5), this is a selective account of events and incidents that are significant in the terms of the genre.

In his prefatory letter Bunyan addresses his readers in terms they will understand, using Scriptural texts, images and metaphors that act almost like a shared language. Similarly in the main body of the text he presents the readers with episodes from his life that are meaningful because they relate to Scripture and to shared assumptions about the nature of spiritual experience. Bunyan selects his material not only on the basis of a personal interpretation of its relevance but also on grounds that are shared with his fellow Nonconformists, that are, in other words, conventional.

Perhaps the most defining difference between Nonconformist churches and the Church of England was the formers' insistence that members make a positive commitment to fellowship. There was no place for those who only maintained an 'outward' show of faith. One result of this view was that the infant baptism practised by the Church of England was rejected as inadequate: a baby or child could not possibly achieve the consciousness of sinfulness and of the need for divine Grace that was necessary for genuine commitment to God. Members of Nonconformist churches would be baptized as adults. One of the conventional ways in which new members of a Nonconformist church would earn or mark their membership was by describing their own experience of conversion in what is known either as a 'conversion narrative' or a 'spiritual autobiography'. These narratives, of which hundreds have survived, generally conform to a pattern that relates the individual's experience to stages of awakening or conversion set out in Scripture. They can also be understood as a significant element of the ongoing process of self-scrutiny that was a distinguishing feature both of Puritanism and of later Nonconformity.

As a Calvinist, believing that individuals had been designated elect or reprobate before birth, Bunyan was aware it was not in his power to know for sure which he was, let alone to alter that judgment, but there was a crumb of comfort in the idea that those who had been chosen for salvation would have consciences that were troubled by their sinful condition, unlike the reprobate who often seemed carefree. The man or woman who had become aware of his or her sinfulness in the eyes of God, or judged against Scripture, would need to search for signs about their spiritual condition.

The search for signs was first and foremost a matter of reading the Bible, the divinely authored text that held the answers to questions about the reader's state. In the same way that incidents and figures in the Old Testament were interpreted as 'types' or foreshadows of those in the New Testament, so the Scriptures contained examples and events that could be matched to the reader's own life. Readers would constantly be identifying with characters or experiences, both good and bad, in order to make sense of their own feelings.

In *Grace Abounding* Bunyan shows how he came to recognize the importance of the Bible. When he is first moved to change his ways as a young man and starts to read his Bible he finds most pleasure in reading the 'historical parts', finding material like St Paul's epistles mean little to him (*GA* 12). It is rather like reading fiction for the young Bunyan, who is only superficially changed, has no sense of the Bible's redemptive project. Then, in one of the best-known passages in the book, he describes an encounter with 'three or four poor women sitting at a door in the Sun, and talking about the things of God' (*GA* 14). Bunyan, who describes himself as a 'brisk talker', listens as they talk about their spiritual experiences. The women speak 'with such pleasantness of Scriptural language, and with such appearance of grace in all they said, that they were to me as if they had found a new world' (*GA* 14). These poor women have experienced the power of divine Grace which transforms their relationship with the Bible. The young Bunyan had read it objectively for pleasure, while it suffuses their discourse, is an active part of their lives.

Bunyan longs to be part of this community of true believers (which is the Bedford church that he eventually joined) and seeks out their company but there are other options and Bunyan, without guidance, is vulnerable to ideas he will later reject. He recounts how he learned to read the Bible 'with new eyes' after the experience of reading some Ranter writings (*GA* 17). Because he was wary of these texts, although they were held in some esteem by 'several old Professors' (declared believers) he prayed to God for guidance: 'Lord leave me not to my own blindness, either to approve of, or condemn this Doctrine' and is helped to avoid temptation and reject Ranter ideas (*GA* 16). He then turns back to the Bible as the one reliable text: 'and indeed I was then never out of the Bible, either by reading or meditation, still crying out to *God*, that I might know the truth, and way to heaven and glory' (*GA* 17). From then on Bunyan turns again and again to the Bible to explain his spiritual condition and throughout his writing, and life, Scripture, correctly interpreted through God's Grace, will be his final point of reference.

One of the most striking features of *Grace Abounding*, and one that has attracted much critical comment, is the active role played by Scriptural verses and phrases. In the young Bunyan's moments of utter despair and anguish Scriptural texts of encouragement will come into his mind and he will search the Bible until he finds them. Others are presented as operating in quite an aggressive fashion at unexpected moments. One 'bolted in upon' him while he was walking by a hedge in the morning (*GA* 40), while another seemed to follow him around: 'Now about a week or a fortnight after this I was much followed by this Scripture, *Simon, Simon, behold, Satan hath desired to have you*, Luk. 22. 31. and sometimes it would sound so strongly after me, that once above all the rest, I turned my head over my shoulder, thinking verily that some man had behind me called to me, being at a great distance.' (*GA* 30) Texts pull Bunyan in different directions, towards depressed conviction of his sinfulness and inevitable damnation or towards a hopeful recognition of God's saving grace. Bunyan, the writer, is keenly aware of the power not only of the Word, but of words.

Bunyan's narrative does not end with a dramatic, or even conclusive sense that he has an assurance of salvation, and it is less systematic than many texts produced by other believers at the time who seem to have followed a pattern laid down in accounts, some in map form, of the stages in the life of the elect and the reprobate. *Grace Abounding* comes to an end with a description of a night when the words '*I must go to Jesus*' fill him with joy and a desire '*for the company of some of God's people, that I might have imparted to them what God had shewed me*' and lead him to Bible verses which God helps him to understand: 'Thorow this blessed Sentence the Lord led me over and over, first to this word, and then to that, and shewed me wonderful glory in evry one of them' (*GA* 74–5).

Grace Abounding is more than a testimony to the power of Grace and the Scriptures. As its prefatory letter showed, this is a text written in response to Bunyan's sense of his calling to minister and preach. He is not merely confessing but offering his life as an example and his readers are asked to examine their own lives for signs, especially of the action of the Word:

> *My dear Children, call to mind the former days, the years of ancient times; remember also your songs in the night, and commune with your own heart, Psal. 77. 5, 6, 7, 8, 9, 10, 11, 12. Yea, look diligently, and leave no corner therein unsearched, for there is treasure hid, even the treasure of your first and second experience of the grace of God toward you. Remember, I say, the Word that first laid hold upon you; remember also your terrours of conscience, and fear of death and hell: remember also your tears and prayers to God; yea, how you sighed under every hedge for mercy. (GA 3)*

This text can be read as a defence of Bunyan's claim to authority as interpreter of the Word, but this can only be maintained by analysing the effects of the Word upon him, as well as his continual efforts correctly to interpret his position in relation to individual scriptural statements and thus within the discourse of salvation as a whole. Bunyan's position must shift between active interpreter of the Word and obedient subject of the Word, between spiritual father of his children and child of God the Father. He is in effect writing a text in order that his own life may be read as God's text: *'Wherefore this I have endeavoured to do; and not onely so, but to publish it also; that, if God will, others may be put in remembrance of what he hath done for their Souls, by reading his work upon me'* (GA 2).

To Bunyan God is the one true author and absolute authority. God's Word, Scripture, has made Bunyan what he is and in transcribing his experience of the power of the Word, Bunyan is offering an example to others of *'the great grace that* God *extended to such a Wretch as I'* (GA 3). His text is to act as a supplement to the Word, not as a substitute. But as with all supplements there is a risk of supplanting the original. In the preface to *Grace Abounding* Bunyan seems anxious about the process of relating the effects of the Word in other words:

> *I could have enlarged much in this my discourse of my temptations and troubles for sin, as also of the merciful kindness and working of God with my Soul: I could also have stepped into a stile much higher than this in which I have here discoursed, and could have adorned all things more then here I have seemed to do: but I dare not: God did not play in convincing of me; the Devil did not play in tempting of me; neither did I play when I sunk as into a bottomless pit, when* the pangs of hell caught hold upon me: *wherefore I may not play in my relating of them, but be plain and simple, and lay down the thing as it was: He that liketh it, let him receive it; and he that does not, let him produce a better. (GA 3–4)*

The association of *'higher'* style and adornment with playing and the assertion of the need to be *'plain and simple'* in relating *'the thing as it was'* suggest a desire to eliminate the dangers inherent in writing. The possibility of incorrect interpretation, of mis-reading, which informs the narrative section of *Grace Abounding* is the cause of a profound anxiety about the narrator's spiritual condition. Yet in offering that narrative as a written account, Bunyan must run the risk of inviting similar mis-readings. This would be a constant anxiety for Bunyan as he struggled to maintain, and to extend, his ministry through the written word and tried to guide his readers to correct interpretation.

If Bunyan had not been arrested but allowed to preach in halls and fields in Bedfordshire and London he might never have felt the need to write directly to the men and women for whose pastoral care he was responsible. He might never have widened his address as time went on to include men, women and children across the globe. But while his turn to writing enabled him to break the silence imposed by the authorities, becoming an author was itself fraught with dangers of far more importance to Bunyan than those to his worldly freedom or security.

4

Bunyan as Writer:
The Pilgrim's Progress

THE AUTHOR'S *APOLOGY* FOR HIS BOOK

Bunyan was kept in the Bedford gaol for twelve years until 1672, when he was released and given a licence to preach. This must have seemed unlikely just a few years earlier when the full force of the Clarendon Code legislation hit home among the Nonconformists of Bedford as church meetings were disrupted and fellow dissenters imprisoned or driven undercover. The tide of persecution ebbed and flowed and imprisonment in the seventeenth century was not like modern incarceration. Harsh and unhealthy though his conditions were, Bunyan's incarceration did not, at first, cut him off from contact with the world. In the very early years he was sometimes allowed visitors, and, when his gaoler allowed it, left the gaol to conduct pastoral visits and even travelled to London to meet fellow Nonconformists. This more lenient regime ended with the Act of Uniformity in 1662 but by 1668, when Bunyan was released on what we would call 'parole', only to be rearrested for not conforming to ecclesiastical law, the mood towards religious dissenters was, if not softening, then modifying. In 1672 the Declaration of Indulgence suspended the execution of legislation punishing those who would not conform to the Church of England, including Roman Catholics and Protestant Nonconformists. While many saw this as a Stuart monarch favouring Roman Catholicism, it heralded a new era when men like Bunyan could not only be pardoned but apply for a licence to preach. Perhaps embarrassingly, given his vehement arguments with them, Bunyan was released as part of what was known as the 'Quaker Pardon'.

Just before his release, Bunyan had been chosen by his church to be their pastor, and the congregation took advantage of the new context of 1672 to buy a barn to be converted into a meeting house. It is clear that by the time of his release Bunyan's standing was considerable not only within his own church but in the regional, and national Nonconformist networks. He helped to apply for a twenty-six licences for ministers to preach in the area and swiftly became the organizing force there. This can have been the only aspect of a nickname he seems to have acquired, 'Bishop Bunyan', that did not seem wholly inappropriate for a man of his religious and social views.

So Bunyan was preacher and writer of note when he emerged from prison in 1672. But would we have heard of John Bunyan today if he had not written the book published six years later, *The Pilgrim's Progress*? The answer should be that some of us probably would: historians of the period and those in the Baptist tradition. *Grace Abounding to the Chief of Sinners* would be rightly celebrated as one of the most vivid conversion narratives of its day and Bunyan's persecution and resilience would be regarded as momentous examples of Nonconformist experience in the seventeenth century. But the fame of this author is inextricably bound to one work and it is perhaps telling that it is, if we are to trust his own words, a work that the committed preacher did not consciously plan on writing.

The Pilgrim's Progress is a text that has been more widely read over a longer period than any other in the English language, except the Bible. Its reach and appeal to diverse readers, as a later chapter will show, has been remarkable and ties its history to that of many cultural and social movements, including those of imperialism and of its resistance, up to the present day. It has been studied and analysed as a great work of literature, praised as an extraordinary example of cultural achievement from the artisan class, and avidly read as an uplifting and improving work in Sunday school and mission house, both in Bunyan's own words and in translation. It has never been out of print and even those who have never read it will know some of its phrases, its settings, and characters: like so many of Shakespeare's phrases, 'the Slough of Despond' and 'Vanity Fair' are part of the currency of English culture. Yet, according to his 'Apology' for the book, Bunyan appears to have started working on the book almost unintentionally, while completing another writing project in prison. In a dramatic description of divinely-inspired creative inspiration, he recalls that he 'Fell suddenly into an Allegory' and that, as he wrote, his ideas 'began to multiply,/Like sparks that from the coals of Fire do flie' (PP 3). Worried that these ideas might 'eat out' the book he was meant to be writing, he concentrated on this new work, not intending it at first for any reader but 'mine own self to gratifie' and 'to divert my self in doing this,/From worser thoughts, which make me do amiss' (PP 3).

The writing process is described as pleasurable and almost effortless: 'Still as I pull'd, it came; and so I penn'd/It down' (PP 3). In this insistence that he had no plan to publish this work is the first hint of an anxiety that is fundamental to Bunyan's attitude to his more 'literary' writing: how to ensure that the artistry that will draw the reader into a compelling narrative does not obscure the serious Christian message to be under-stood. Bunyan had been writing for twenty years and always faced the threat of misinterpretation but, although he had already demonstrated a lively turn of phrase and sure touch with homely analogies in his sermons and treatises, the turn to a full-length allegory, a story which has much in common with worldly adventure stories, would mark him out as a great writer, but might that be at the cost of his Christian mission? Would his readers miss the, doctrinal, point?

The Romantic writer and critic Coleridge famously commen-ted that in The Pilgrim's Progress, 'his piety was baffled by his genius, and the Bunyan of Parnassus had the better of the Bunyan of Conventicle'.[1] This assertion that Bunyan's imagina-tion operated in conflict with his religious purpose and faith may have been intended as a compliment to a timeless literary genius, understood in early-nineteenth-century terms, but it would have horrified the seventeenth-century writer. A majority of critics and scholars have since insisted that this opposition of Parnassus and Conventicle is not apposite when trying to understand Nonconformist, and wider religious, writing in Bunyan's age. There is not a scrap of writing by Bunyan, including letters, that has survived that is not written in the service of his Christian purpose, few metaphors and analogies that do not tie his texts to the Scripture where he found the examples, and direct 'permission' he needed to use language to its fullest capacity to reach and help redeem an ever-wider readership. As N. H. Keeble has noted, the Puritan, and later Nonconformist, culture of which Bunyan was part 'was a pre-eminently social movement whose considerable literature was characterized by a fascinated interest in the actual experiences of men'.[2] In this community of writers and readers, engaging with the everyday life of the world, with its pleasures and perils, and understanding that experience in terms of faith, and the journey to salvation, made the stuff of life material for religious enlightenment.

But, as Bunyan's preface to *The Pilgrim's Progress* shows, the author anticipated, and discussed with fellow believers, the risks that this new work, with its entirely allegorical narrative, might do more harm than good. He recounts the arguments for and against publication, drawing on scriptural and worldly examples, to justify his method, claiming that the divinely-authored Bible sets the key precedent: 'By Calves, and Sheep; by Heifers, and by Rams;/ By Birds and Herbs, and by the blood of Lambs;/God speaketh to him: And happy is he/That finds the light, and grace that in them be' (*PP* 6). Gradually, as he counters possible arguments against his method, his tone becomes more defiant and exhortation to the reader more direct. This is, he claims, a book that will 'profit' the reader, one with serious intent that will, if properly read, help the reader on his or her own journey to salvation: 'This book will make a Travailer of thee,/If by its Counsel thou wilt ruled be;/it will direct thee to the Holy Land,/If thou wilt its Directions understand' (*PP* 8). The reader then is warned that they must learn from this book, that this is no mere fable, but as the preface builds to its conclusion, calling on those who enjoy riddles, or 'picking meat', to 'be in a Dream, and yet not sleep', the emphasis is joyously on the pleasures of reading (*PP* 8): 'Wouldest thou loose thy self, and catch no harm? And find thy self again without a charm?/Would'st read thyself, and read thou know'st not what/ And yet know whether thou art blest or not, By reading the same lines? O then come hither, and lay my Book, thy Head and Heart together.' (*PP* 9) It is hard to imagine a more enticing appeal to a readership for whom the question of whether they were 'blest or not' could be a real torment.

Bunyan's misgivings about his allegorical method, and the conflicting views of others, may be one of the reasons why *The Pilgrim's Progress* was not published for some years after he finished writing it. It has proved hard to pinpoint the exact dates of writing, because records are few, but it is evident that Bunyan wrote the book in prison. The critical consensus is that Bunyan probably wrote, or completed, it during a second six-month period in Bedford gaol from December 1676 to June 1677. Bunyan had been active as a preacher and organizer, as well as writer, since 1672, and had continued to conduct written debates with other Nonconformists as well as treatises. It is possible that Bunyan began the allegory as a free man but once again, persecution would lead to production. Bunyan's second imprisonment followed the withdrawal of the Declaration of Indulgence and cancelling of the preaching licences granted under its terms; although this was in part caused by fears that the king's brother and heir was a Roman Catholic, it led to a renewal, and intensification of persecution of Nonconformists. Bunyan was released after the intervention of influential Nonconformists, but the extra time in prison, while undoubtedly a time of suffering, afforded him another space for writing. His imprisonment and suffering for not conforming, together with the powerful resistance his writing constituted, frame the allegory, and the image of the dreamer in the 'Den' in the opening sentence, glossed in the margin as 'The jail', is as enduring as that of Christian with his burden (*PP* 11).

The Pilgrim's Progress was first published in 1678, by the London printer Nathaniel Ponder, who published many Nonconformist works, and as W. R. Owens has noted, Ponder may have spotted the book's potential, as he obtained a licence for it, giving him copyright.[3] Ponder was right: eleven more editions were published before Bunyan's death ten years later and the book became an instant bestseller. It is only possible to see why by actually reading the text itself, but this chapter will explore some of its distinctive features.

The fact that Bunyan's writing would attract serious literary criticism centuries later, is something of a reproof to at least one of his most dismissive contemporary critics and to those who repeatedly sneered at his lack of formal education and manners. In the 1670s, particularly in the years just before his release from gaol, Bunyan had been engaged in an energetic exchange of combative treatises with what are known as Latitudinarian Anglicans, representatives of the Church of England who defined themselves against what they saw as the extremes, in belief and practice, of 'high-church' fellow Anglicans and radical Nonconformists alike.[4] As his writings, from *Grace Abounding* to his allegories, show, Bunyan was as vehemently opposed to this respectable position as he was to the antinomianism he saw in Quakers. In 1670 Edward Fowler, the Rector of Northill, a parish near Bedford, wrote in defence of what he termed reasonable religion and in opposition to Calvinist beliefs in a treatise called *The Principles and Practices of certain Moderate Divines of the Church of England* and the year after in *The Design of Christianity*. Bunyan responded in 1672 with *A Defence of the Doctrine of Justification by Faith* and the dispute continued. Although both men were ardently championing deeply held religious positions and the robust language used in treatises reflected this, Fowler and his supporters were also disdainful of Bunyan's style and learning: in the anonymous *Dirt Wip't Off* Bunyan was denounced for, among other things, 'brutish barkings', 'ignorant fanatic zeal', and 'insufferable baseness'. Bunyan's social, educational, and religious shortcomings are seen as interconnected and as grounds for dismissing his claims to write with any authority.

Bunyan always made a virtue of his lack of formal education, even exaggerating it, linking himself with a proud tradition of inspired rather than trained religious thinkers. It is, however, gratifying that when he attempted an ambitious re-working of a great literary tradition, the allegory, his success would ensure that he would be celebrated for his cultural contribution while Fowler is generally encountered in footnotes.

The Pilgrim's Progress is, as Bunyan's preface states, an allegory, written in the once-popular form, rarely used after the development of the novel, in which, as their names indicate, characters and places represent abstract ideas or qualities and the overall narrative explores a universal rather than particular story. The full title of the work *The Pilgrim's Progress from This World to That Which Is To Come* signals the ambitious scope of the work and the real destination of the protagonist. The 'progress' of Christian is not just the journey of one man but represents the experience of the Christian soul from conversion to salvation and the names and places the reader encounters remind him or her of that universal, and personal, dimension of the story. Reading allegory can be a rather remote, intellectual experience, especially for those used, as modern readers are, to realist fiction; the demands of personifying qualities or ideas can strain the credibility of characters and limit our emotional response. Yet in *The Pilgrim's Progress* Bunyan balances the 'representative' status of his characters with realist and naturalist detail and dialogue that has encouraged many critics to see it as a direct forerunner of the novel.

The story is framed by a conventional device of a man who dreams the allegory that follows, but adapted by Bunyan, as already described, to represent the prisoner/author. Some readers might already have encountered Bunyan's treatises or other early works, perhaps even *Grace Abounding*, but the opening paragraph of this new book immediately establishes a dramatic, and realistic, tone that will make this very different.

CHRISTIAN'S PROGRESS

The dreamer sees 'a Man cloathed with Raggs', with 'a Book in his hand, and a great burden upon his back' (*PP* 10). This is man, burdened with sin, encountering divine truth in the Bible. As the dreamer watches, the man reads and cries out: 'as he Read, he wept and trembled: and not being able longer to contain, he brake out with a lamentable cry: saying, *what shall I do?*' (*PP* 10). So from the very start the reader is gripped by the portrayal of a man whose reactions and personality seem both particular and real. The man, later to be named Christian, may be a personification but he is also a person. Throughout the text, Christian's thoughts and feelings before, during, and after, his adventures and challenges create a sense of psychological immediacy while the dialogue draws the reader into a world where social distinctions are as carefully delineated as doctrinal differences.

Christian's story starts with his flight from his home City of Destruction when he learns from his Book (the Bible) of the inevitable death and damnation to come because of the Burden (of sin) he and its other inhabitants bear, here presented as a literal burden on his back. This poor man, clothed in rags, is called Graceless (as the text reveals later on), but he is, for all his sinfulness, one of the elect, predestined to a hard struggle that will end in salvation. Graceless is counselled by the pastor figure, Evangelist, to head for the Wicket-gate and towards the shining light beyond. Carrying a 'Parchment-roll' given to him by his adviser, on which is written 'Fly from the wrath to come', he heads off only to be called back by his wife and children: 'but the man put his fingers in his Ears, and ran on crying, Life, Life, Eternal Life' (*PP* 13). Bunyan is following scripture here and the margin refers the reader to Luke 14. 26 on the necessity of putting God before all worldly ties: 'If any *man* come to me, and hate not his father, and mother, and wife, and children, and brethren, and sisters, yea, and his own life also, he cannot be my disciple'. Here, as throughout the text, the dramatic action, like the dialogue and contemplation, is dictated by Scripture. But it is the fingers in Christian's ears that communicate the heart-rending choice that must be made by each believer who would be saved, and that point to Bunyan's skill in choosing the telling detail that brings his characters to life and makes *The Pilgrim's Progress* such a vivid story. As the man makes the agonizing choice to leave his family behind and seek salvation, and defends his decision to his neighbours Obstinate and Pliable, he is given the name of Christian.

Christian's ensuing adventures are instructive but they are also exciting: his journey matches the stages and experiences of conversion and the search for salvation, but each scene is depicted with a vividness that makes theological topography seem grittily genuine and personifications of spiritual conditions as real as our neighbours. On his way to the Gate Christian finds himself enmired in the 'Slow of Dispond' or Slough of Despond (*PP* 17), here a literally boggy area that stands for the doubts and fears that accompany a Christian's awakening to his or her sinful condition. This is a landscape that its contemporary readers will have recognized as that of rural and small-town England, depicted in sensory detail that captures the pleasures and the miseries of a spiritual journey through their physical counterparts.

One of the first characters that Christian encounters is the urbane Mr Worldly-Wiseman, an inhabitant of the neighbouring town of Carnal-policy. Assured, aloof, and dismissive of Evangelist's message that Christian must suffer trials and privations to be saved, Mr Worldly-Wiseman is both the personification of the doctrine of works (that argued moral behaviour rather than total reliance on divine Grace could lead to salvation) and a convincing character who patronizes the anxious and socially inferior Christian. Like other broadly amiable but theologically misguided characters, Mr Worldly-Wiseman is a character Christian must learn to reject, as the book's readers must in their own encounters with them in real life. It is perhaps in this depiction of judgments against those who seek the easy way, or only partly follow God's law, that some modern readers find the greatest challenge in *The Pilgrim's Progress* as the case of the character Ignorance, discussed later in this chapter, shows most clearly.

Christian travels through a world that blends the giants and monsters of epic tales with the recognizable social settings of the market fair and the country road. This is a journey fraught with dangers on every level: the everyday risks that would have threatened a man or woman walking in seventeenth-century England, from sloughs to footpads; the agents of persecution, personified here in characters like Mr Hate-light and Mr Implacable, who targeted Nonconformists like Bunyan; the failings and flaws of the individual Christian, here externalized as characters like Giant Despair. Together these threats make up the dangerous world through which (the) Christian must travel towards the world to come. But the world and its perils cannot be the only, or even the main, focus for the Christian seeking salvation. Christian must learn to interpret his experiences as part of his essentially *spiritual* condition, and so must the reader.

Bunyan's notes in the margin regularly draw the reader's attention to the key point or meaning of an episode or to a scriptural reference, and act as visual reminders that the reader should be concentrating on learning from the text, without undermining the narrative's pace and tension. The reader is also shown Christian learning to interpret in the key scenes in the House of the Interpreter, which he visits early on his journey when he feels the burden of sin is weighing heavy. Here

Christian is shown pictures and scenes that work rather like the emblem books that were popular in the early-modern period and is shown learning from these examples. Comforted and reinvigorated, he runs on until he finds a hill on which stand the cross and the sepulchre, denoting Christ's sacrifice for humanity's salvation. There his burden falls off and he is re-clothed, marked on his forehead, and given a roll impressed with a seal, to be given in at the Celestial Gate. These marks of spiritual condition all have scriptural origins but the roll will also feature as a device that builds tension when Christian loses, then finds, it along his way.

Christian's story is one of eventual, and difficult, triumph over enemies that often combine several layers of significance. Soon after losing, then re-finding his roll, Christian is welcomed in the Palace Beautiful, which stands for the congregation of the faithful. There he discourses with Prudence, Piety, and Charity, the daughters of the Lord of the Hill, who offer him instruction and support. When Christian leaves to face the dangers of the Valley of Humiliation he has been armed with the sword, and armour, of the spirit. The man who was once clad in rags is now equipped, despite his fears, to battle the 'foul Fiend' (*PP* 55). Apollyon, whose appearance, 'with scales like a Fish (and they are his pride)', 'wings like a Dragon, feet like a Bear', 'mouth of a Lion' and belly that breathed fire and smoke, linked him to traditional monsters, was named after one of the angels of Hell in Revelations, and so represents the devil's power (*PP* 57). But in his speech and conduct we also see him as a figure of worldly, or state, authority, as he refers to himself as 'Prince and God' of the City of Destruction and Christian's 'King' (*PP* 57). This is not a simple, anti-Royalist characterization; in *The Pilgrim's Progress*, as elsewhere in his writings, Bunyan is more concerned with the attitude of rulers to God and the godly than to their status. In his battle with Apollyon Christian is confronted by the choice between obedience to ungodly, antichristian state power and authority and his greater duty to his true Prince, Jesus. Here, as throughout the story, elements from different registers – scriptural, political, everyday – combine to dramatic effect.

Delivered, by God's grace, from his battle with Apollyon, Christian travels through the Valley of the Shadow of Death with its terrifying spectacle of the Mouth of Hell, surrounded by fiends, and fearsome groans, and blasphemous whispers. At the end of the valley, sustained by his faith, Christian is able to pass by a cave where two giants, Pope and Pagan used to live. Here Bunyan gestures out of the frame of the narrative to the history of persecution, suggesting that change is possible, and adds a welcome touch of humour as he depicts the Pope who has 'grown so crazy and stiff in his joynts, that he can now do little more than sit in his Caves mouth, grinning at Pilgrims as they go by, and biting his nails, because he cannot come at them' (*PP* 66).

Bunyan's depiction of the physical and social world of the narrative is strikingly vivid; everyday settings and objects bring his theological points to life, often have a satirical or humorous edge, and are, above all, recognizably realistic. This is a world where dogs bark when you knock at the door and pilgrims' legs ache on the journey. If such a world resembles the reader's own, the lessons told must also apply. The telling details that convince us that Christian's experiences were designed to be understood and recognized by 'ordinary' men and women give the allegory a dramatic immediacy and a realism that anticipates the novel. Although the story is framed by the device of the narrator's dream, we experience it almost as a play, but one where we must be wary of making easy judgments about the characters we see and hear. As one editor notes, we rely remarkably little on the narrator for information in *The Pilgrim's Progress*: instead we witness characters in dialogue, with all the misunderstandings and challenges such encounters entail, for the reader, as well as for Christian.[5] Bunyan's eye for detail, in appearance and in dialogue, allows him to create convincing characters whose moral or religious flaws are subtly signalled to the attentive reader in give-away phrases or habits. As Christian learns to understand and assess those he encounters, so too must the reader. This gives the allegory much of its hold on the reader's imagination but also its rigour as a teaching text that tests rather than lectures.

Christian has travelled alone until he emerges from the Valley of the Shadow of Death, when he meets a fellow pilgrim Faithful. The men agree to travel together, discussing their experiences on their journeys, and testing their beliefs, as well as their ability to assess, in encounters with characters like the entertaining, and outwardly religious, but spiritually empty

Talkative whose departure is marked by a wonderfully matter-of-fact marginal note: 'A good riddance' (*PP* 82). A meeting with Evangelist reminds the men of the 'Crown of life' that awaits them but warns that 'one or both of you must seal the testimony which you hold, with blood' (*PP* 85). Aware of the trials to come but also the ultimate reward, the two men enter the town where one will be martyred.

The scenes that follow present Bunyan's clearest dramatization of the treatment of Nonconformists in a hostile world; they also demonstrate, through biting humour, his criticism of the rich and powerful. The world depicted here is one where commerce and social snobbery dominate. In the Fair, the market held in the town of Vanity, the reader is shown a vivid depiction of a world where everything is for sale including 'Preferments, Titles, Countreys, Kingdoms, Lusts, Pleasures, and Delights of all sorts, as Whores, Bauds, Wives, Husbands, Children, Masters, Servants, Lives, Blood, Bodies, Souls, Silver, Gold ' (*PP* 86). The apparently indiscriminate mixing of commodities, people, and even souls suggests the amorality of the contemporary socio-economic world from Bunyan's perspective as well as the longer, broader context of a fallen, sinful world. Pilgrims like Christian and Faithful 'must needs go thorow this Fair', as Christians must live in the world, but their appearance and speech mark them out as different: 'Some said they were Fools, some they were Bedlams, and some they are Outlandish-men' (*PP* 87). When the pilgrims are asked what they want to buy, they reply '*We buy the Truth*' (*PP* 87); like Bunyan in his own trial insisting on interpreting the notion of 'calling' as a religious one rather than a matter of worldly occupation, Christian and Faithful counter the language of the market with that of faith. In both cases this conflict of words results in the punishment of the Nonconformists after a trial in which there is no place for justice.

The reality of persecution experienced by generations of Puritans and Nonconformists pulses through the depiction of Vanity Fair. The episode in which Christian and Faithful are apprehended and put on trial, the latter brutally executed and Christian providentially escaping, combines elements of the shocking and the comic. In the trial scene social standing and moral vice distinguish the 'worthy Gentlemen' who witness against the pilgrims and pack the jury, deliberating on the two men's guilt with no pretence of justice (*PP* 94). These men are the personification of sins and vices – Mr Blind-man, Mr No-good, Mr Malice, Mr Love-lust, Mr Live-loose, Mr Heady, Mr High-mind, Mr Enmity, Mr Lyar, Mr Cruelty, Mr Hate-light, Mr Implacable – but their opinions, prejudices, and voices resonate with those who condemned Bunyan himself. Here, as in the depiction of the amorality of the town's marketplace, the implacable, if sometimes veiled, hostility of the socially ambitious and worldly towards the faithful and the godly, is presented with humour as well as bite. These men are being mocked, as they sneer.

The men are both found guilty and while Christian is remanded in prison for some time, as Bunyan had been, Faithful is condemned to die. His protracted sufferings echo the terrible cruelties described in texts such as Foxe's *Acts and Monuments* which reminded Nonconformist readers of the harsh realities of persecution across the ages (*PP* 95).[6] It was, however, a reality to be endured. Brutal punishments and execution were, of course, still meted out to Nonconformists, as Bunyan's experience, and fear of execution related in *Grace Abounding*, testified. Yet, even as the horrors of persecution are acknowledged, the blessings of salvation are offered as a comfort. In the allegory, immediately after Faithful's terrible physical torments, culminating in being burnt at the stake, are described, the author adds: 'Now, I saw that there stood behind the multitude, a Chariot and a couple of Horses, waiting for Faithful, who (so soon as his adversaries had dispatched him) was taken up into it, and straightway was carried up through the Clouds, with Sound of Trumpet, the nearest way to the Coelestial gate.' (*PP* 95)

Christian escapes to continue his progress but he is not alone. A new companion, Hopeful, who has been moved by witnessing the sufferings of the pilgrims in Vanity Fair, reassures the reader that enduring persecution and suffering may encourage others to seek salvation. Christian and Hopeful continue their progress towards the Celestial City, encountering other realistic yet representative characters, such as Mr By-ends, who 'always had the luck to jump in my Judgement with the present way' (*PP* 98). They travel through a landscape including the dangerous 'By-Path Meadow', whose softer going tempts weaker pilgrims from the straight and narrow, leading them not to salvation but to the 'Pit' (*PP* 108). They are captured by Giant Despair who imprisons them in 'a very dark Dungeon, nasty and stinking to the spirit of these two men' (*PP* 110). This stinking dungeon is in 'Doubting-Castle' and the dramatic tension of the pilgrims' physical peril is more than matched by the intensity of the exchanges between them as Christian starts to succumb, as Bunyan once did, to the sin of despair. If the Vanity Fair scenes capture the parallels between the fictional characters and seventeenth-century Nonconformists, the episode of Doubting Castle dramatizes the potentially damning misery of doubt and loss of hope. Hopeful encourages Christian in his despair but it is the protagonist who recalls 'I have a Key in my bosom, called Promise', which he uses to free both men from their captivity (*PP* 114).

The men travel and converse, learning from their experiences, and reflecting on their beliefs until they eventually reach a River, representing death, that stands between them and the Celestial City. The experience of death is depicted as difficult, particularly for the more fearful Christian, who wrestles with his terrors and can barely keep his head above water, with Hopeful's aid. Here, as in Faithful's martyrdom, Bunyan does not ignore the fearsome realities of necessary suffering, but again assurance of divine support is immediate. When, eventually the men reach 'the other side' of the river, a marginal note reassures the reader, 'Angels do wait for them so soon as they are passed out of this world' (*PP* 149).

Christian and Hopeful are met by the Heavenly Host and taken, through a Gate that reminds the reader of Christian's first point of entry to this journey, into the Celestial City that represents their salvation. There they are 'transfigured' in a joyful celebration of man and angels united in praise for God and the Dreamer interrupts the narrative to comment: 'And after that, they shut up the Gates: which when I had seen, I wished myself among them' (*PP* 153).

If *The Pilgrim's Progress* ended here, the reader would be left with a wonderful vision of salvation that they too might wish to share. But it does not. The Dreamer turns away from the vision of the Celestial City to see what happens to a minor character who the pilgrims had encountered on their journey: Ignorance.

Ignorance, a young man from the Country of Conceit,

described himself to the older pilgrims as 'a good Liver': 'I Pray, Fast, pay Tithes, and give Alms' (*PP* 120). In conversation with the pilgrims he outlines his own faith in justification, and eventual salvation, through obedience to God's Law and Duties: 'Christ makes my Duties that are Religious, acceptable to his Father by virtue of his Merits; and so shall I be justified' (*PP* 140). Ignorance believes that he can walk a 'fine, pleasant, green Lane' (*PP* 120) of faith because Christ has sanctified his actions or works and so he will be saved. In this he recalls the earlier figure, Mr Worldly-Wiseman, who trusts in good works not divine grace. He keeps apart from Christian and Hopeful who are walking the harsher path of faith in salvation through Christ's own righteousness alone and rejects their attempts to teach him, calling their beliefs 'whimzies' (*PP* 141).

The last stages of the young man's journey to the next world are as smooth as Christian's were difficult: he is helped across the river by a ferryman called Vain-hope and walks confidently to the gate to enter the Celestial City. There, having no Certificate, he is bound hand and foot and carried off from the very Gates of Heaven to Hell. This is the last vision of the Dreamer: 'So I awoke, and behold it was a Dream' (*PP* 154).

The decision to end the narrative not with the salvation of Christian but with the damnation of Ignorance is instructive. Some modern readers find Ignorance's fate harsh but Bunyan's depiction of the consequences of his failings is a vital part of the allegory's mission to instruct and to save. Ignorance has put his faith in fulfilling the religious duties defined in the region of his 'Countrey' as the way to be saved (*PP* 120). But, like those who followed the established rituals, obligations, and required acts, of the Church of England, according to Bunyan's theology, he has mistaken a good life for true knowledge of saving grace. His is, in Bunyan's terms, damnable ignorance and it is of the greatest importance that readers are not so swept away with the joy of Christian's salvation that they overlook the dangers of complacency. Complacent belief in an outwardly religious, or morally impeccable life, ignores the reality that faith in divine grace is the only means to salvation. The example of Ignorance, and his damnation, prevents the narrative from achieving a neat closure and reminds the reader that the journey of faith is never easy.

THE CONCLUSION

The critic Arnold Kettle suggested that a persecuted minority will not only express its faith in allegorical terms as a tactical strategy but because 'its *thinking* will be in those terms'.[7] This is an appealing idea and Bunyan's allegory certainly offers models for thinking of the challenges and sufferings of the Christian life in ways that do not romanticize but honour the struggles of men and women who were too often sneered at as well as persecuted. But like Christian's experience in the House of the Interpreter, the process of reading an allegory is one which Bunyan feels the need to circumscribe with warnings.

Bunyan's dramatic narrative and dialogue that carries the reader along, is effectively framed by guidance on how to read and interpret the action. The prefatory apology had set the interpretative scene and marginal signposts prompted the reader to pause and reflect. This frame is completed in 'The Conclusion'. This is a brief verse afterword, after the allegory is concluded with the word 'Finis', a Latin term that perhaps sits oddly in Bunyan's emphatically plain style. The Dreamer warns the reader against paying too much attention to the 'out-side *of my Dream*', and urges him or her to look beneath the metaphors: 'There, if thou seekest them, such things to find,/As will be helpful to an honest mind' (*PP* 155). It would be a reckless reader who, after seeing the fate of Ignorance, chose to ignore Bunyan's warning against complacent reading. It is only after this reminder of the way the book should be read that we see the words, in good plain English: 'The End'.

It was not, of course, the end of *The Pilgrim's Progress*. The book was an immediate popular success and, as a later chapter will show, its journey into other land and different times has given it one of the greatest and most diverse histories of books that have changed the lives of their readers. It had an impact also on the standing of its author who swiftly gained a literary fame that held little meaning for Bunyan but has lasted through changing fashions in reading and in the conventionally-accepted canon of English literature. After the publication of *The Pilgrim's Progress*, the book's title was included on title pages of his works in editions from different publishers. The Bunyan who had hitherto been best-known as a preacher, even if

45

encountered in written form, as in *Grace Abounding*, was now best, and most widely, known as 'the author of The Pilgrim's Progress'.[8] Reading the text as literature is, of course, if not antithetical, then tangential to Bunyan's intent. It is an irony that although there are many readers who continue to read *The Pilgrim's Progress* for its core Christian message, many others are drawn precisely to the 'out-side', to the skilful and engaging narrative that brings seventeenth-century social, cultural, and theological worlds so compellingly to life. Yet books have always exceeded their author's control and readers read differently both from each other, and as their own contexts and priorities change.

Bunyan ended his final verses with a note that if the reader 'cast all away as vain', 'I know not but 'twill make me Dream again' (*PP* 155). In this tempting threat we may see a hint of the sequel to Christian's story that is usually published with the original in modern editions and that traces the journey to salvation of his wife and family. But Bunyan did not return to the City of Destruction as depicted here until 1684. The year after *The Pilgrim's Progress* was published the formally conventional, if powerful, *A Treatise of the Fear of God* appeared, but Bunyan had clearly been working on another allegorical story, published in 1680, which is the immediate sequel to *The Pilgrim's Progress*.

5

The Life and Death
of Mr Badman

The shining success of *The Pilgrim's Progress* in its own day and
since, whether viewed in terms of popularity, literary, or
pastoral achievement, inevitably obscures Bunyan's later works.
Whether or not the second part of the allegory is regarded as a
separate work or as a companion piece, the story of Christian's
pilgrimage and that of his fellow travellers has a unique place
globally within the history of English literature. Yet Bunyan's
mission to write for an ever-wider and more diverse readership,
in order to aid their own journeys to salvation, led him to
explore other literary forms in works that have much to reward
the attention of modern readers interested either in the period
in which they were written or the history of literature. The
favourable reception of *The Pilgrim's Progress* had a notable
impact on Bunyan. Although he continued to write treatises and
sermons, and to be actively involved in his own church affairs,
as a later chapter will discuss in the context of a controversy
over women's worship, his fame led to calls to preach ever
further afield and his confidence in the effectiveness of his
literary experiments grew. Bunyan would always be anxious
about misinterpretation and would insist on God's sole absolute
authority but his own growing assurance as an author is
notable.

The Life and Death of Mr Badman, published in 1680, was
presented by Bunyan as what we might in modern parlance call
a 'follow-up', as opposed to a formal sequel. In his customary
address to the reader, the author noted that as his story of the
progress of 'the Pilgrim from this World to Glory' had proved
'acceptable to many in this Nation', it had 'come into my mind

to write, as then, of him that was going to Heaven, so now, of the Life and Death of the Ungodly, and of their travel from this world to Hell' (*MB* 1). He goes on to explain that he has chosen to tell this story in the form of a dialogue 'that I might with more ease to my self, and pleasure to the Reader, perform the work' (*MB* 1), and calls on the reader to examine his or her own life to see 'whether thou thy self art treading on his path' (*MB* 1).

The text presents the life of an utter rogue, reprobate in theological terms and villainous in everyday life. His life is recounted by two men whose names, Wiseman and Attentive, signal their status as reliable commentators whose conversation explores the lessons to be learned from the example of Badman. Their names would fit easily into the allegorical world of *The Pilgrim's Progress* but the form and style of this book is very different, calling on established narrative traditions and, at times, foreshadowing the novel to come. The dialogue model had been used in one of the books that influenced the young Bunyan, Arthur Dent's immensely popular *The Plaine Man's Pathway to Heaven* (1601), and firmly establishes the instructive purpose of the book with the dialogue serving as a dramatic sermon. Yet throughout the text Wiseman and Attentive also relate graphic, and at times shockingly violent scenes that are not from the life of the fictional Badman. These are, as marginal notes indicate, stories from real life, including cases witnessed by the author. The scenes show God's judgment at work directly in the world, with sinners experiencing the full, violent force of divine punishment and were popular in texts, known now as 'providence' or judgment literature, that combined instruction and sensation. An influential example of the period, and source of some examples used here, was Samuel Clarke's *A Mirrour or Looking-Glass to Both Saints and Sinners* (1671). We cannot know how Bunyan's original readers reacted to these stories but their apparently true status and shock value contribute to the text's disjointed but compelling narrative. Between the extremes of sermon and sensation sits the grim tale of Mr Badman himself.

Mr Badman is presented as a character in a vividly drawn urban world which its contemporary readers would have recognized as their own and this is the feature of the text that has drawn the most attention from literary critics, including some who have argued that it deserves recognition as a

forerunner of the realist novel.[1] He is an exemplary figure but he
also lives in a recognizable world and behaves in recognizable,
if reprehensible, ways. Badman's life story is told by the two
commentators who leave the reader in no doubt about his
sinfulness from an *'ominous'* beginning as a child displaying all
the signs of 'Original Corruption' (*MB* 17). It is easy to imagine,
as contemporary readers must, that this rogue trader might
have been found on the streets of Bedford or any other English
market town.

Mr Badman's life is both individual and exemplary, a tale to
be followed and a lesson to be learned. In the preface Bunyan
claims that 'England *shakes and totters already, by reason of the*
burden that Mr. Badman *and his Friends have wickedly laid upon it'*
and Wiseman's decision to recount the story of Mr Badman to
Attentive is prompted by the latter's concern about the 'badness
of the times' (*MB* 2, 13). The times were indeed bad for
Nonconformists as persecution of religious dissent intensified
in the aftermath of the Popish Plot, a fictitious conspiracy fed by
anti-Catholic fears; not only was the religious climate oppressive
but the high Tory culture, marked by sexual and material
indulgence, typified by the fashionable world of Restoration
theatre, appeared to be in the ascendant. England truly seemed
to be a world of amoral excess. But, as usual, while Bunyan's
criticisms of the rich and privileged hint at a connection between
material success and moral corruption, his emphasis is on
religious redemption rather than social or political change *per se*.

Wiseman notes that it is 'bad men that make bad times' and
that nothing will improve while 'sin is so high' until, through
God's work, sinners repent (*MB* 13). This repentance itself is
seen to have a positive impact on a man's behaviour and so on
others. While the text does not contradict the idea of
predestination or of the primacy of grace, and never deviates
from Bunyan's conviction of the inability of good works to affect
one's salvation, its focus on the vital need for sinners to repent,
and on the social aspects of sinfulness, suggest that behaving
well in the world is the duty of the Christian man, woman, and
child. Here, as in Bunyan's earlier treatise on proper conduct,
Christian Behaviour (1663), a careful way is steered between the
libertarian, even libertine possibilities of predestinarian theology, as interpreted by antinomians like the Ranters, and the

excessive stress on outward signs of holiness and good works of the established church. Mr Badman may have been designated damned from before his birth but in his life, and refusal to repent, lessons can be learned that apply to individuals and to their communities. This is a book for Christian readers living in the world and seeking guidance on how to navigate its dangers. The fact that Mr Badman seems to relish many of the same amoral pleasures and pursuits that were associated with Restoration high society suggests that Bunyan's readers may also be encouraged to take a view on the fashionable amorality of their 'betters', but his middling class and setting in a small town ensure that his story hits 'home'.

Mr Badman's story is a catalogue of sins and crimes that connect breaking God's Law with cruelty and abuse of other people. We are told that his sinfulness was evident from childhood, when his lying, stealing and Sabbath-breaking grieved his parents; we learn that he was apprenticed to two masters, was set up in a shop, and as an adult indulged in swearing, drunkenness, and keeping the company of similarly sinful young men. After a rather lurid exploration of his indulgence in 'whoredom', when Bunyan through his commentators, expounds particularly on the evils of 'whorish women', Badman's sins extend to a pretence of holiness that is intended solely to entrap a young Christian orphan whose fortune is transferred to him on marriage.

The narrative has been likened to that of later picaresque novels, in which a hero or anti-hero moves from adventure, or misadventure, to another, but Badman rarely attracts our sympathy. His victims, however, do, even if they are given little psychological 'life' on the page, as Badman's behaviour is chillingly described. Recalling the drunken husband's return home late at night, Wiseman notes '[I]f his wife did but speak a word to him, about where he had been, and why he had so abused himself, though her words were spoken in never so much meekness and love, then she was Whore, and Bitch, and Jade; and 'twas well if she miss'd his fingers and heels' (*MB* 70).

The account is both matter-of-fact and convincing. Here, and throughout the text, connections can be made, and have been noted by many critics, with Bunyan's experience as a leader in his own church.[2] As pastor of his congregation, Bunyan had responsibility for dealing with the everyday conduct of church members, including disagreements and lapses from expected Christian conduct. *The Church Book of Bunyan Meeting* is a collection of entries, many in Bunyan's handwriting, many of which record the misdemeanours of local people, from Sabbath-breaking and brawling to wife-beating and the disciplinary action taken by the Church Meeting in each case. The similarities between many of Mr Badman's sins and crimes and those of the people of Bunyan's own congregation and community, signal that this text both draws on the realities of its potential readers' lives and confronts them with the wickedness of what might seem social rather than religious misdemeanours.

The scope of Badman's wickedness also extends, significantly, to his commercial practices. We do not learn what his shop sells, as we would in a novel, but we do learn that he is guilty of many forms of sharp business practice including usury and engineering a false bankruptcy to evade his creditors. Badman's approach to work, and to business, is defined by his amoral greed; he exploits the market economics of early capitalism without conscience or concern for the repercussions of his actions. It has been argued that the text features the debut of Hobbesian man, defined by ruthless material self-interest, and while the dialogue never challenges the idea of market economics, the example of Badman's exploitation of its rules and practices, and the lessons drawn for its readers, suggest that proper conduct in commercial matters was a challenge taken seriously in Nonconformist communities.[3] The implication of this text in debates that linked the social and theological is also evident in discussion in the text about whether or not Badman was an atheist which have been shown to contribute to, then contemporary, debates about atheism and the relationship between unbelief, reprobation, and damnation.[4]

To return, as Bunyan's text does, to the story of Mr Badman, his life may be a catalogue of sin and crime but it is, in material terms a success story. There are some reversals of fortune and even one episode where after breaking his leg in a fall from his horse he appears briefly to mend his ways only to return, on recovery, to his old ways, like 'the Dog to his Vomit' (*MB* 140). The lesson here is that 'sick-bed fears' are no grounds for true repentance and in the story, the dashing of false hopes proves too much for Badman's wife, who goes into a decline and dies. The shameless Badman announces, with characteristic and convincing crudeness, that he will not seek a replacement : *'Who would keep a Cow of their own, that can have a quart of milk for a penny?'* (*MB* 145). But this time he meets his match and is amusingly lured into marriage by a woman who 'would give him Oath for Oath, and Curse for Curse' (*MB* 145).

In due course, Badman succumbs to a host of diseases, including 'a tang of the Pox in his bowels' and Consumption, and the reader is prepared for the death scene promised at the start of the text (*MB* 148). Badman's death is accompanied in the text by one of the longest and certainly the most gruesome and distressing exchanges of sensational 'real-life stories' by Wiseman and Attentive. These are accounts of suicides, including that of John Cox of 'Brafield by Northampton', a poor man who became sick, worried he could not work, and 'fell into deep despair about the world' (*MB* 159). Cox's suicide, which included disembowelment, is related in graphic detail, and is given as a warning against his implicit rejection of God, revealed in his refusal to pray for forgiveness for his forbidden, and theologically damning, act of suicide. The scenes, and lessons drawn from them, shock modern readers and seem almost sadistic, yet they also serve to foreground one of the most important parts of Badman's story. In contrast to the terrible, bloody and painful deaths of men driven to Godless despair, Mr Badman dies quietly in his bed 'like a Lamb' (*MB* 161). The violent, abusive, cheating villain drifts from life without apparent pain or fear. But he dies without repenting and so, far from ending his sinful life at peace or in Grace, 'he is gone to Hell and is damned' (*MB* 162). This quiet death is final.

The Life and Death of Mr Badman was not as popular as *The Pilgrim's Progress:* only three editions were published in Bunyan's lifetime and there are no references to it in his later work to give any sense of its reception. Most critics see it as flawed, or limited, in literary terms, and it is undoubtedly less assured and compelling than *The Pilgrim's Progress*. The lengthy instructive passages seem alien to most modern readers at least in the context of a 'story' as do the cautionary examples of men and women whose despair seems to be an understandable reaction to poverty but is here judged as damnable. Yet they would have been differently received by readers immersed in, or at least familiar with, the conventions of providence or judgment narratives, who may have been more surprised to find a credible story of one reprobate man connecting them. These reminders of the very real differences between modern readers and those to whom the text was addressed make this a text to consider rather than enjoy. It would be misleading to label this as a novel in the making, but the creation both of the world in which Badman lives, a convincing society of shopkeepers, inns, apprentices and merchants, and of a character whose utter badness is leavened by flashes of psychological realism and humour, points to Bunyan's real literary skill. Just as he does in the sermons and treatises that earned him a loyal following of ordinary men and women, Bunyan captures the world and the speech of those people in phrases and exchanges that enliven even his most determined rejection of worldly values.

6

The Holy War

In 1682 Bunyan returned to allegory, publishing *The Holy War*, a history of 'the Town of Mansoul'. *The Holy War* is arguably the most atypical of Bunyan's works in form: an ambitious, multi-level allegorical epic that is grander and apparently more detached in style than his earlier writings. Bunyan's prose is still, at its best, distinctively colloquial and warmed by the imagery and diction of rural and small-town life of the period, but the structure is certainly more elaborate and his authorial stance less overtly personal. As the editors of the Oxford University Press edition of the text note, the author is 'no longer the dreamer, but an observer'.[1] Yet this stylistic detachment and literary complexity belie the fact that this is, like its predecessors, a committed text with a redemptive purpose: a story to engage, and entertain, its readers as a means to call them to repentance and, God willing, to salvation. This simple fact is one that has all-too-often been overlooked, or undervalued, in critical readings and evaluations of the text since its publication. Bunyan's position as author is never detached. One critic has rightly observed, that Bunyan's stance in *The Holy War* is that of the prophet and, while the literary qualities of the allegory are notable, this prophetic engagement with the times and destiny of its readers alone makes it worthy of attention.[2]

Bunyan's second allegory dramatizes what Roger Sharrock called 'the second great metaphor of Christian experience', turning from pilgrimage to warfare, but as in *The Pilgrim's Progress*, his subject is the struggle for redemption.[3] This story, as grimly entertaining as it is, is offered to the reader as an alternative to 'vain stories' because 'Til they know this, [they] are to themselves unknown' (*HW* 1); it is as much the story of a soul as Christian's journey.

The Holy War is an allegory of the history of an individual soul, here presented as a city, Mansoul, created by King Shaddai (God the Father), that is repeatedly besieged by the forces of Diabolus (Satan), and granted hope of salvation by Shaddai's son Emanuel (Jesus). Bunyan draws on his own experience and skill to create a vivid narrative of military manoeuvres and battles that faithfully dramatizes the historical sweep of Scripture from the fall of Lucifer to Christ's incarnation and it gestures prophetically to the final judgment that lies beyond the end of the allegory. He painstakingly presents each stage of the biblical narrative in military action that also stands as a metaphor for the psychological stages and experiences of the individual, with his ever-useful marginal notes directing the reader's attention to scriptural grounds or meanings.

The first assault on Mansoul is, as it is in Milton's earlier *Paradise Lost*, an act of revenge on the part of the fallen angels, when God's favoured creation, mankind, is attacked and corrupted. Here the city of Mansoul is literally besieged by the forces of evil, led by Diabolus, as the individual soul is beset by them, and the epic story invites the reader to interpret the story on both levels. Each of these dimensions – the entirety of Christian history and the individual soul – is universal and, in contrast to *The Pilgrim's Progress* and *The Life and Death of Mr Badman*, the text has an epic scale and structure that makes this a sweeping rather than an intimate narrative. Yet some features of the story, and of Bunyan's style, connect it to the world of his seventeenth-century readers and prevent it from becoming too remote. The story is one of a violent, war-torn world – 'Mansoul, *it was the very seat of war*' (*HW* 4) – that must have been all-too-familiar to readers who had lived through the terrible years of civil conflict and the turmoil of their aftermath. Bunyan also, through the conceit of visiting Mansoul 'even till I learned much of their mother-tongue, together with the Customs, and manners of them among who I was', creates a world that is believable even if the narrative is less psychologically intimate than his earlier allegories (*HW* 7).

Bunyan's subject is universal and the allegorical presentation of the human soul in conflict has its roots in biblical and early Christian writings.[4] But *The Holy War* is also conducted on terrain that closely resembles the author's native land and one level of the allegory tracks the dramatic political changes that affected the lives of Puritan and Nonconformist men and women throughout his life. The period of *The Holy War*'s composition and publication was marked by particular turbulence, with vehement struggles between emerging political factions (Whig and Tory) that focused on what each saw as the greater threat to the established order: for the former, Catholics, including the king's own brother and heir, James, for the latter, Nonconformists such as Bunyan. After 1678 the discovery of the alleged (and almost certainly imagined) Popish Plot to kill Charles II testified to, and heightened, growing hysteria about the threat of religious nonconformity. In what is known as the 'Exclusion Crisis', attempts by the emerging Whig group to pass a parliamentary bill excluding Catholic succession to the throne, were countered by Charles II using royal prerogative to dissolve Parliament to block it and by the Tory group urging the rigorous implementation of laws against Nonconformists. Upheavals at court and in national government must have alarmed people for whom the traumas of the civil war and revolutionary period were far-from-distant memories, but the impact of renewed persecution was felt throughout a still-divided nation.

The political, and polarized, debates of the period were conducted in vehement argument in text and pamphlet but also in literary works, as writers took sides. Tory, royalist works included John Dryden's satirical *Absalom and Architophel* (1681) and although *The Holy War*'s marginal annotation repeatedly encourages the reader to consider it as an allegory of spiritual conversion, its allusions to the political world resound in the context of persecution and fear of the period. The trauma of the civil war would have been in many adults' memories and its tumultuous aftermath had given some groups little peace. In one of the works not published in his lifetime, Bunyan described the period after the Popish plot as one of real terror 'then we began to fear cutting of throats, of being burned in or beds, and of seeing our children dashed in pieces before our faces', but he also noted that 'a gracious king, brave parliaments, a stout city, good lord-mayors, honest sheriffs, substantial laws' had buttressed the people against the threats.[5] In *The Holy War* both are dramatically evident, as are characters whose responses to the repeated changes of regime in Mansoul reflect not only the spiritual conditions of their allegorical role but also the complexities of human behaviour in wartime and its aftermath.

So, the brave Mr Conscience, the town Recorder who resists Diabolus, is compromised, like his fellow townsmen, by his failings in keeping true to King Shaddai, but is also 'a man of courage and faithfulness to speak truth at every occasion: And he had a tongue as bravely hung, as he had a head filled with judgment' (*HW* 18). Threatened by the Recorder's oratory, when the old man's conscience-driven speeches rouse the town against its new ruler, Diabolus adopts a twofold strategy, to tempt him into sin and debauchery and to convince his fellow men that he is mad. Mr Conscience, submitting periodically to a temptation that undermines his position, becomes unsteady and embattled but retains his ability to stir up his fellow Mansoul residents and 'by the power of *Shaddai*, and his wisdom, he was preserved' (*HW* 21). Lord Willbewill, in contrast, standing for the Will, values his social standing so highly that he places himself in the service of Diabolus 'being stated and setled in his places, offices, advancements and preferments; oh! you cannot think unless you had seen it, the strange work, that this workman made in the Town of Mansoul' (*HW* 22). Conscience and Will play different parts in the Christian understanding of individual psychology but Mr Conscience and Lord Willbewill also come to life as contrasting characters responding to the stresses, and opportunities, of conflict and change.

Mansoul's history echoes the tumult of the English Revolution and Restoration on a national scale, summarized, with apt merging of real and allegorical dimensions by Christopher Hill, as 'from the Anti-christian tyranny of Charles I and his bishops, through the all-too-brief rule of the saints, to the return of Diabolus in 1660, and his ultimate overthrow'.[6] *The Holy War* is an epic allegory of conflict, within the soul and within local and national politics. It has often been noted that Bunyan's experience in the army must have helped him to create vivid scenes of military campaign and warfare: the battles and sieges follow convincing patterns and echo with the sounds of warfare like the '*Hell-drum*' that 'beat most furiously' (*HW* 200); the punishments of the defeated, whether women 'forced, ravished, and beastlike abused' by Diabolonians (*HW* 204), or the gruesome, but scripturally grounded executions of the

Diabolonian Doubters and Bloodmen when King Shaddai is restored, dramatize the effects on a human soul but ring true when read as human suffering in wartime; one critic has noted that King Shaddai's great captains – Boanerges, Conviction, Judgment, and Execution – would not have looked out of place in the New Model Army.[7] So while marginal notes help the reader interpret the action in terms of an individual soul, the drama unfolds on a bloody, epic scale.

The story is not only one of armies and sieges; the war between good and evil, the struggle to live a Christian life was conducted in peacetime as well. Mansoul's history is also that of the towns and cities of Bunyan's England, including Bedford, which were the subject of draconian and, to Bunyan, anti-Christian legislation and intervention at the period when he wrote *The Holy War*. A town run by tolerant men might be a more sympathetic place for Nonconformists than a rural village where magistrates often favoured the local gentry and established order. In the Restoration, the rigorous imposition of the Corporation Act, intended to strengthen the hold of crown and established church over municipalities that were seen to tolerate dissent, had brought dramatic, unwelcome change to Bunyan's home town. His local experience adds a dimension of social realism and political comment to the allegory, as Bunyan interweaves the story of civic politics with that of military campaigns. The negotiations, compromises, and civic politics of Mansoul, recall the 'new-modelling' of corporations like Bedford and dramatize a feature of contemporary life that would have resonated with Bunyan's first readers. Might not there be a Mr Conscience or a Lord Willbewill in a town like Bedford too?

Bunyan's skill in weaving together the different strands of his allegorical narrative without sacrificing too much in pace or convincing setting is considerable. The topography of Mansoul is one that a reader would recognize from the period. It has been connected, persuasively, by Richard Greaves, with London, which must have helped the seventeenth-century reader to draw comparisons, for example, between the courts of Diabolus and Charles II.[8] But to keep the allegory of the struggle for salvation of an individual human being in play, that topography also connects with the body: the besieged city, for example, has gates that contemporary readers would have seen in walled, or once-walled, cities in England, but the names Ear-Gate, Eye-Gate, invite them to think of the individual's experience.

The city is similarly peopled by characters who connect the different strands of the allegory. Some are personifications of human attributes and qualities, such as Mr Understanding, Mr Conscience, Mr Forget-Good; others represent divine or diabolic figures, including the Lord Chief Secretary, who stands for the Holy Spirit; others closely resemble figures from contemporary history, such as Mr Filth, a Diabolonian appointment who publishes lewd ballads and songs and bears an uncanny resemblance to Roger l'Estrange, licenser of the press under Charles II, and a determined opponent of Nonconformist publishers and writers.

A notable feature of *The Holy War*, and one that unites all its allegorical levels, is its attention to rhetoric, to the power of crafted speech to persuade for good or ill. This is a war of words as much as of physical force. Diabolus is depicted, not unlike his counterpart in Milton's *Paradise Lost* (1667), and perhaps like Charles II, as a charismatic orator, able to exploit his audience's baser instincts, and Emanuel is shown to recognize the importance of recapturing 'Ear-Gate' in his efforts to free Mansoul. The key characters' voices are distinctive and contrasting in content and syle. Diabolus's speech is manipulative, as in the scene where he attempts to exploit his listeners' fear of King Shaddai and to persuade them that their self-interest would be best served by staying loyal to him: 'But consider I say, the ball is yet at thy foot, liberty you have, if you know how to use it: Yea, a king you have too if you can tell how to love and obey him' (*HW* 63). Emanuel's words, resonant with scriptural reference, are more direct, stating his cause and calling on Mansoul: 'O *Mansoul*, neither is my Commission nor inclination at all to do the hurt; why flyest thou so fast from thy friend, and stickest so close to thine enemy?' (*HW* 76). The allegory culminates in a five-page speech by Emanuel after the Diabolonians have been defeated and the town is at peace but still searching for dangerous figures like Mr Unbelief. It is a speech that relates the story of the preceding action from Emanuel's perspective but also builds into a powerful call to the reader who must by now be in the position of Mansoul: 'Nor must thou think always to live by sense, thou must live upon my

Word' (*HW* 250). It is fitting that a text that has dramatized the importance of speech and hearing, words, and the Word, in the battle for salvation, should end in a speech by the character representing Jesus that seems to break the bounds of the allegory to address the reader. The final words, neatly if not deliberately, recall Bunyan's earlier epic, as Emanuel says: 'Behold, I lay none other burden upon thee, than what thou hast already, hold fast till I come' (*HW* 250).

There has been some critical debate about the conclusion of *The Holy War*, with some commentators judging it to be ambiguous, and others holding it to be entirely consistent with Scripture.[9] If read within the context of Bunyan's own theological position, the last part of the text seems entirely appropriate to his mission: the narrative may end but the story of Mansoul cannot be concluded except by God. It has recently been noted that *The Holy War* is not only the most neglected of Bunyan's 'literary' works in studies of his writing but has been repeatedly marked by successive generations of editors and critics as, to varying degrees, a failure.[10] While Bunyan's second extended allegory has never achieved the popularity of his first, the judgment that it fails may reveal more about the aesthetic, cultural, and political assumptions of the critic than about the text, as *The Holy War* is expected to conform to literary or hermeneutic models that are alien to the text's and author's purpose and framework of belief. It is certainly a less compelling narrative in terms of characters with whom to identify or a story that stays in the memory, but its ambition, multiple layers of meaning, and fusion of the types of battle that dominated the seventeenth-century in England reward our reading still.

7

The Pilgrim's Progress:
The Second Part

The author's introduction to the original *The Pilgrim's Progress* started as an apology for his form and method, only gradually building in confidence as he reminded the reader of his many scriptural precedents. His tone as he presents the second part in 1684 is quite different. Although Bunyan had published *The Life and Death of Mr Badman* as the sequel to his first hugely successful allegory to limited success, other writers and publishers had seized the opportunity to provide follow-up volumes designed to appeal to the public. Some, like Thomas Sherman, a Baptist writer who published a sequel in 1682, made no pretence to being the author of the original, but others, as Bunyan claims in the preface to *The Pilgrim's Progress: The Second Part* and in a poem published with *The Holy War*, either pretended to be, or hinted that they were, him. Bunyan, who had made no claim to literary as opposed to pastoral ambitions, is keen to expose these 'fake' sequels and to establish his authorship. In the new preface, Bunyan addresses the book as a text but then conflates it with its female protagonist, 'my Christiana' in a tone that is confident and protective (*PP II* 139). It is a combination that distinguishes the narrative itself and connects with two topics that have attracted much critical interest: Bunyan's growing authorial confidence and his representation of gender.

Bunyan's preface reassures Christiana/the book, who voices possible obstacles to a positive reception, by describing the success of *The Pilgrim's Progress*. This gives him an opportunity to list both the range of countries where the book has been a success, including France, Flanders and New England, and the type of readers, differentiated not only by age, from children to adults, but also by class. Unusually for Bunyan, who rarely describes the social, as opposed to godly, elite in positive terms, he lists 'Brave Galants', and 'Young Ladys, and young Gentlewomen too' among those who have read and valued the book (*PP II* 137). This account of the appeal of his earlier book is followed by a description of each of the main characters in this sequel from Christiana and her family to '*old* Honest', '*Master* Fearing', '*Master* Feeblemind', and '*Master* Despondencie'. The passage acts as a taster, hinting at characters and events to appeal to the prospective reader, but it also introduces a key feature that distinguishes this new volume from its precursor.

While the first allegory traced the story of one man, Christian, who despite his companions and encounters, embarked on his pilgrimage alone, this will be the story of a group of people. It will also be about people who, by virtue of age, gender, physical or moral weakness, are far from conventionally heroic. Their story will be one of effort, mutual support, and dependence on the guidance offered both by the charts and tokens that stand for the scriptures and by protective figures like Great-heart. It is a story that, as many critics have noted, is well-suited to the slightly more settled times of the Nonconformist church in the mid-1680s when persecution had abated somewhat. Although incidents like the Rye House Plot, an alleged Republican uprising, triggered draconian punishment and revealed the continued deep divisions in society, in this period Nonconformists could focus on other concerns. In Bunyan's new book the virtues of godly companionship in church communities and the efforts of those facing the challenges of their own weakness and sin rather than external threats and persecution, take centre stage in a depiction of a new journey that is as domestic as it is dramatic.

The narrative, once again framed as a dream, returns to the question of what happened to Christian's family when he left them behind to seek salvation. Here Christiana, his wife, is beset by a conviction that it was her fault that her husband left. As she says, memorably, to her children: 'I have sinned away your father and he is gone' (*PP II* 146). While Christian's decision to leave his family behind was entirely consistent with scriptural teaching, Bunyan's vivid depiction of the man with his fingers in his ears to block out their cries conveys the emotional wrench of rejecting the family. Now Christiana takes full responsibility for her husband's decision and her belief that she has sinned in this way is a major part of the impetus that leads her to follow his pilgrim's path to salvation. Her conviction of sin here replaces the physical burden that her husband carried but bears the same weight as the starting point of spiritual awakening.

Christiana follows the same route from the City of Destruction to the Celestial City but her journey differs in two main ways. First, she travels with a group: she takes her children and a younger woman, Mercy, who asks to join her, and as she progresses is joined by other characters who stand for the infirm, the weak, and the fearful, as outlined in the preface. As this group assembles and travels together, under the guidance of their protector Great-heart, they form a Christian community that learns to support its members. Second, the route that Christiana follows is topographically similar to that travelled by Christian but his actions have altered it in significant ways and the new pilgrims are able to apply the lessons of his experiences when they face the same challenges and threats. As N. H. Keeble has noted, it is in this second part, where the later pilgrims comment on Christian's earlier feats, that the heroic aspect of his conduct is established: in the original text the emphasis was on his own fallibility, but here a newer group with even less confidence in their own physical and, most of all, spiritual strength, cast him as hero.[1] So the reader who has been encouraged to identify with the all-too-human fears and anxieties of the lone male pilgrim is here invited to see how his example offers support and encouragement to others. Individually, and together, the two parts of *The Pilgrim's Progress* dramatize and extol the virtues and benefits of shared experience and community that act as vital counter-balances to the self-examination and individual responsibility of Calvinism. In the stories of the pilgrims and their mutual support and learning we see imagined ideals of the Bedford women in the sun who appealed to the anxious young Bunyan.

The question of how Bunyan depicts women and of his own attitude towards them, and to gender relations in his time, has exercised many critics and scholars and is an obvious theme for studies of this second part. Perhaps predictably, the depiction of female characters in this, and in Bunyan's other narrative texts, is more complex, less easily reduced to the stereotypical, than in his doctrinal and didactic treatises. Two of these treatises, *Christian Behaviour* (1663) and *A Case of Conscience Resolved* (1683), reveal something of Bunyan's views at different stages in his life as well as the combination of scriptural and social forces that shaped them.

Christian Behaviour closely resembles the popular conduct manuals that offered guidance on how households were to be run. Here Bunyan's emphasis is on godly conduct and the text derives its model of appropriate roles for individual members of the family and for their relationships from scriptural sources. Bunyan presents a conventional patriarchal model, with the husband and father as head of the household. In his section on 'The Duty of Wives', he is uncompromising in his assertion that the woman 'ought in every thing to be in subjection to him, and to do all she doth, as having her warrant, license, and authority from him' (*MW III* 32). As the references to warrant, license, and authority suggest, Bunyan draws an analogy between the relationship of the wife to the husband and the church to Christ and, while the subjection of the wife is absolute, he insists that he does not 'intend women should be their husbands slaves' (*MW III* 34). In *The Life and Death of Mr Badman*, Bunyan depicted, and condemned, the sufferings of a godly woman subjected to abuse by a reprobate husband, but in *Christian Behaviour* he warns that even a woman who has married a *'froward, peevish and teasty'* unbeliever or *'a sot, a fool'* must 'take heed of desiring to usurp authority over him' (*MW III* 34, 36). So, while author and reader's sympathies may be drawn to the wife abused by her husband, the scriptural foundation and social structure places her under his authority. Husbands are advised against abusing that authority but wives, and women, are, in essence, to be guided by men. In their personal conduct they must also beware of having an *'idle, talking* or *brangling tongue'*, 'a wandring and a gossiping spirit', *'immodest apparel'* or *'wanton gate'* (*MW III* 33). It is easy to see negative depictions of female immodesty and improper behaviour in Bunyan's narratives where lascivious and vulgarly dressed women stand for carnal or worldly excess but what of the godly women who, in the later seventeenth century, were claiming a new, public role in the service of God?

A Case of Conscience Resolved, published twenty years later, shortly before the second part of *The Pilgrim's Progress* offers an intriguingly different perspective on Bunyan's involvement with women. It is his first, and only explicit, engagement with the demands being made by women in the period for a position from which to speak publically on religious matters. Before he became a minister, the young Bunyan had been intrigued by and drawn to the Bedford women who sat together in the sun speaking of God and testifying to the power of Grace but in the 1680s, as leader of a congregation, he felt the need to speak out against a group of women who felt that they were moved to meet for worship separately from men. Bunyan's response is a treatise that assumes that his otherwise well-behaved female church members have been encouraged to establish a practice he condemns by a rival minister, Mr K, usually identified as William Kiffin, a London-based Baptist with whom Bunyan clashed on numerous matters. In contrast to his exchanges with Quakers, where Bunyan is distancing himself from their theological, and implicitly political, position, his disputes with Kiffin show the ways in which Nonconformists of broadly similar doctrinal positions felt the need to differentiate themselves on matters that reveal the social dimensions of their beliefs.

In a text that is responding to women seeking a more active part in church affairs, or one where the men to whom they are to defer are not present, Bunyan effectively excludes their voices, and agency, by addressing the male minister to whom he ascribes the idea. He claims, in paternalist terms, to be acting for their *'Honour and good order'* and upbraids Mr K for his *'Boldness* in *Fathering* his mis-understanding upon the Authority of the Word of God' (*MW IV* 296, 299). He also, tellingly, extends his condemnation to women having any public voice within the church and its meetings. The women's request was for limited involvement in contrast to the actions and texts of many more assertive figures of female spirituality in the period, from the outspoken prophets of the revolutionary period, to women like the Quaker Margaret Fell whose *Womens Speaking Justified* (1667) offered Scriptural readings that countered, and modified, those used to silence her gender. Fell was imprisoned in the year that Bunyan published *A Case of Conscience Resolved* amid renewed persecution of dissenters following the discovery of the Rye House Plot and Bunyan is keen to differentiate his, and his congregation's, position and views from those of the more socially disruptive sects, explicitly saying that he cannot support women ministering 'to God in prayer before the whole Church, for then I should be a Ranter or a Quaker' (*MW IV* 305). The treatise has been described, by Christopher Hill, as 'a remarkably explicit assertion of male ascendancy' and certainly Bunyan's position as minister, responsible for maintaining discipline within his church as well as offering spiritual guidance, is conservative in its understanding of the role of women and uncompromising in its insistence on their proper subservience.[2]

The combination of the two treatises suggests that Bunyan was conservative in his view of the position of women. Far from sharing the radical interpretation of their possible role in God's service promoted by some Nonconformist groups, he is anxious to reassert an interpretation of Scripture that denies them the type of socially unconventional agency for which he had already been persecuted by the secular authorities. This, coupled with the depiction of sinful, secular women who tempt and torment godly men, suggests a less than appealing attitude to women, but is it a fair, or complete, picture of Bunyan's engagement with women in his writing?

There are a number of examples in Bunyan's own writing of women speaking and acting in public in ways that might seem improper if judged by his pronouncements in his treatises.[3] In 1683 he noted that even those who believed in women's meetings would not send a woman to petition the king for their lives (*MW IV* 308) and yet in the account of Bunyan's own trial it is related that his wife petitioned for his release. Her actions are presented as appropriately feminine and on his behalf, but she addresses the judges in a direct, accusatory manner that bears little resemblance to the modes of female speech commended in *A Case of Conscience Resolved* and *Christian Behaviour*. The account was not published until 1765, and while there are many reasons why it would have been politically dangerous to print the relation of his imprisonment, the depiction of his wife's role might also have sat uneasily with his developing public discourse on women.

Considering what Bunyan's private views on women may have been, and whether they differed from those he expressed in his treatises can lead to no conclusions but some evidence suggests that, in common with other ministers, he was subject both to the pressure to maintain order and to accusations that he abused his position. *Grace Abounding*'s account of his call to ministry includes a vehement denunciation of rumours and accusations of womanizing, culminating in the extreme assertions, 'it is a rare thing to see me carry it pleasant towards a Woman' and '[T]heir Company alone, I cannot away with' (*GA* 85). The passage is conventionally associated with the case of a young woman called Agnes Beaumont who travelled with Bunyan to a meeting and was subsequently accused of murdering her father. Beaumont was acquitted and wrote a fascinating account that, as well as being a spiritual autobiography, dramatically shows the difficulties she faced in trying to reconcile conflicting loyalties in a patriarchal society: to her father who disapproved of her church-going and to her spiritual father-figure, Bunyan.[4] The narrative refers to, and rebuts, rumours that there was an improper relationship between the married minster and the young female member of his congregation and while Bunyan never directly commented on the case, it seems likely to be at least one of the rumours listed in *Grace Abounding*.

Whatever his personal views of women, as a minister Bunyan was caught up in a web of relationships that potentially set him at odds with the gender relations of everyday social life. As spiritual and pastoral leader of a church that might expect a man or woman to leave behind their unbelieving or unconvinced wives or husbands to seek their own personal salvation, the accusation that a minister was seducing a woman away from her proper subjection to her husband's authority was always a possibility. In such circumstances it is not difficult to see why a minister, such as Bunyan, might feel the need to stress his belief in and strive to maintain, socially conservative gender relations. Where they mirrored those in his own interpretation of St Paul's understanding of proper female conduct, which emphasized public silence and conformity to male authority, this will have been more a matter of mission than expediency.

It is intriguing, in either case, that it is in the second part of

The Pilgrim's Progress, published soon after *A Case of Conscience Resolved*, that Bunyan devotes the most space and time to delineating female characters and to considering their paths to salvation. Is he redressing the balance after asserting the need for traditional gender roles in his church? Is he presenting acceptable versions of female godly behaviour? Is he responding to female voices querying Christian abandoning his family? We cannot know the answers, or if the questions were asked, but as a literary text, the allegory inevitably offers a less doctrinaire representation of women.

Here the main female characters, Christiana and Mercy, epitomize both traditional female virtues and weaknesses, and some of their experiences, notably the intimidating encounters with 'ill favoured' ones (*PP II* 146–7, 160) which resonate with physical menace as well as spiritual threat, and which reinforce their social vulnerability. Both women, as a widow and as an unmarried woman, are in positions that mean they are not immediately subject to the authority of a husband. In contemporary English society this could afford women some independence depending on their means, but here Bunyan swiftly places them in the care of a man. Although they embark on their journey without male 'protection', they are soon accompanied by the figure of Great-heart who is often likened to an idealized pastor, who battles with giants but also offers spiritual instruction; so the main part of their journey, and their agency, is circumscribed by appropriate male guidance. Under this guidance, female characters are seen to offer each other mutual support, typified by Mercy's devotion to the older woman, to show courage as well as compassion and, in the scene where Prudence chastises Christiana's children, the good mother is presented as offering worthwhile instruction.

Much has been written about the more domestic tone and setting of this text, in contrast to the first part, but this should not be overstated. Certainly, there are numerous homely images and analogies, notably in the 'Significant Rooms' whose emblematic images including spiders and hens and chicks, seem to be designed to appeal to the children, as they will in Bunyan's later collection *A Book for Boys and Girls*. When the party arrives at the House of the Interpreter they are taken to the rooms because supper is not ready, which adds a charming touch of realism, and elsewhere scenes of family life as Christiana's sons grow up and marry, do give the text a strong social dimension (*PP II* 164). But this narrative is marked by harsher moments too and even the character of Mercy, whose conduct generally personifies softer female virtues, displays tougher views. When she expresses a longing for a looking glass, it is easy to see this as an example of stereotypical feminine vanity, but this mirror is glossed as the 'Word of God' in which the reader sees herself (*PP II* 240). Earlier, this character has also confounded modern, if not seventeenth-century, expectations associated both with her gender and her name.

When the pilgrims encounter the hanged bodies of Simple, Sloth, and Presumption, it is Mercy who says *'let them hang and their Names Rot, and their Crimes live for ever against them'* (*PP II* 177). To emphasize her point she expresses it again in song. Unlike Mr Valiant-for-truth's song, it is not one that has been turned into a hymn. This may be addressed to readers in a slightly less tumultuous period than the earlier allegory, but its characters are still governed and shaped by a tough creed. The theology that insisted on the damnation of Ignorance will also ask the reader to accept that Mercy is not sweet tolerance. In these doctrinally necessary moments of tougher conduct and discourse we might hear faint echoes of the female voices Bunyan would not, or could not, allow in his own church. These echoes are, of course, produced by the text as read in our own context and from a modern perspective that sees the place of women in society as politically, and morally, significant. Whatever his pastoral responsibilities and personal views, such matters cannot have been of paramount importance to Bunyan.

Although this second allegory of pilgrimage explores community and companionship, and recognizes a society, epitomized in the return to Vanity Fair, which is 'more moderate now than formerly' (*PP II* 229), matters of worldly existence, whether gender relations or even the persecution or good conduct of the godly, are of fleeting importance when compared to the central tenets of Bunyan's faith. The intricate cruelties of Faithful's martyrdom may have been succeeded by less overtly violent threats, but the perils of despair and of neglecting to follow Scripture, are still the godly's greatest challenge; guidance, from Scripture, and from minister, is to be taken, but the work to be done is for each man or woman. At the end of this text, each of the main party of pilgrims is called for by death and travels individually over the river to the Celestial City and salvation. In the final scenes witnessed by the narrator, we are shown the 'Horses and Chariots' that had appeared to mark the salvation of the martyred Faithful in the first allegory, and we are told that Christian's children have also 'gone over' (*PP II* 290), so this is a culmination of life's pilgrimage that is a shared experience.

Yet arguably the greatest impact on the reader of the moving end of this second pilgrimage is in the words of Mr Stand-fast, a character who some readers might have overlooked or forgotten, as indicated by a reminder in the text that he was encountered by the pilgrims 'upon his knees in the *inchanted* ground' just a few pages before the conclusion (*PP II* 288). There is a structural parallel with the focus, at this culmination of the journey, on another apparently secondary character, Ignorance, in the first part of *The Pilgrim's Progress*. But while Ignorance's smooth crossing to damnation is a warning to the reader to avoid complacency, Mr Stand-fast can be read as a positive example of the imperfect, suffering and fearful, yet determined Christian. After the others in the party have crossed over the River, he is summoned, and, calling on Mr Great-heart to send word back to his family of his own, and Christian and Christiana's 'Blessed Condition', reminds the reader of the necessarily individual nature of the search for salvation. As he stands in the, once-terrifying but now calm river, this ordinary man's words are profoundly moving as he reflects on his journey and the blessings of Christ in words that echo scripture but are also personal and direct:

> I have loved to hear my Lord spoken of, and wherever I have seen the print of his Shooe in the Earth, there have I coveted to set my Foot too. His name has been to me as a Civit-Box, yea sweeter then all Perfumes. His Voice to me has been most sweet, and his Countenance, I have more desired then they that have most desired the Light of the Sun. His Word I did use to gather for my Food, and for Antidotes against my Faintings. He has held me, and I have kept me from mine Iniquities: Yes, my Steps hath he strengthened in his Way. (*PP II* 289)

This eloquent reminder of the intimate relationship between the individual and Christ, voiced by a character who is both marginal and central, ordinary and 'called', encourages the reader to focus on his or her own relationship with Christ and his Word. The good society of fellow Christians is a blessing but salvation is a matter for the individual and God alone.

Yet the broadening of appeal to, and targeting of, particular groups or types of reader that Bunyan had started with *The Pilgrim's Progress* and made explicit in the preface to this sequel, would be developed further in his next, and last, literary work. While, in the end, worldly matters of social or even biological status are of little importance in relation to the fundamental matters of conviction of sin and the search for salvation, Bunyan continued to refine and extend his attempt to bring ever more readers to the Word through his words.

8

A Book for Boys and Girls

A Book for Boys and Girls may be viewed, from one modern perspective, as the culmination of Bunyan's attempts to use his abilities *as a writer* to appeal to, engage, and encourage an ever-wider and more diverse, readership to seek salvation. It has, however, attracted the least critical attention of all his literary works. This is, in large part, because it was addressed, not only but directly, to children. One Bunyan scholar who has written about it notes that Bunyan's best-known impact on the history of children's literature is as the author of *The Pilgrim's Progress* and, as the next chapter will show, the allegory became a Sunday school staple in the centuries following the death of the author.[1] Yet it is this last literary work to be published, in 1686, before his death that Bunyan explicitly wrote for children, as well as adults, and it deserves attention both as a contribution to writing for children and, I would argue, as the culmination of his own approach to the role of writing in pastoral work. It also exemplifies many of the characteristics that distinguish Bunyan's writing as a whole: his commitment to, and skill in, appealing to his readers with images and metaphors they will understand; his use of older, popular literary and cultural forms and traditions in the service of reaching new readers; and the ever-present challenge of encouraging attentive, rather than indulgent or wayward, reading.

Here Bunyan returns to the foundation of his Nonconformist Christian faith's attitude to the role of reading in each human being's search for salvation; *personal, attentive* reading of Scripture is at the core of Protestant and Nonconformist belief and in *A Book for Boys and Girls: Or, Country Rhimes for Children* Bunyan adopts a twofold strategy to helping spread the reading of the Word. The main body of the text comprises seventy-four poems, of varying lengths, that encourage readers to see examples of the work of God in the ordinary, everyday things they would see in the world around them. Fish and ants, spiders and dung heaps all feature in poems that may, in many cases lack technical precision, and rarely match Bunyan's energetic grace in prose, but have a charm and immediacy that endures. The everyday world of seventeenth-century England that provides the convincing setting for the dramatic journeys of *The Pilgrim's Progress* is now the primary focus of Bunyan's literary vision of the divine in the mundane.

The collection recalls the popular emblem book tradition, an early-modern form that combined written text and visual image to convey religious or moral messages. Early emblem books invited the reader to consider, even meditate upon, the relationship between often quite complex allegorical images and scriptural texts in order to deepen their religious understanding and experience.[2] It is widely accepted that the scenes in the Interpreter's house in both volumes of *The Pilgrim's Progress* dramatize the experience of considering the meaning of emblematic scenes but *A Book for Boys and Girls* is not a simple continuation of the tradition. This volume does contain a few simple woodcut illustrations but the majority of poems stand alone, creating vivid images in the reader's mind but, more significantly, deriving their subject matter directly from the everyday world that would have been familiar to children. Some of the poems are divided into a descriptive stanza and a 'Comparison' that draws out the religious message but most integrate image and explanation and the illustrations here appear to be reinforcing the poems' meanings.

Bunyan's subjects range widely but always stay within the grasp of the child reader. Some explore features of the natural world, following scriptural precedent in drawing analogies between the behaviour of animals, the time of day, even the weather, and spiritual or moral conditions. While the subjects are simple, the poem's meanings are rarely simplistic. As Shannon Murray has noted in her careful reading, poems such as 'Meditation upon Peep of day', 'Upon a low'ring Morning', 'Upon the Suns Reflections upon the Clouds in a fair Morning' and 'Meditations upon day before Sun-rising', play on multiple layers of analogy between 'sun' and Son (of God) and can be interpreted sequentially as a spiritual progression. Many poems use animals as examples. The ant, scripturally and proverbially associated with industry, is presented here as offering a shaming example to human beings; in 'Upon the Pismire', a title which tellingly uses the colloquial name for the ant, the reader is told that 'Man's a Fool,/Or silly Ants would not be made his Guide' (*MW VI* 241). Building on scriptural precedent for seeing the spiritual lessons to be drawn from the lowliest of animals, Bunyan chooses many that would have been familiar to most, if not all, of his readers, including spiders, larks, snails, moles, fish, butterflies and frogs.

Some poems focus on what would have been familiar features of life in the country or town, from objects like candles, dung heaps and spectacles to fishing and fowling. Here Bunyan's delight in music and in bell-ringing, that earlier in his life caused him great anxiety as he searched for the answer to how these pleasures might fit the Christian life, are presented as a source, carefully enjoyed, of proper pleasure to please God; two poems even offer simple notation, encouraging children to explore music. This lighter tone is always tempered by seriousness of intent and by a pervading message that sin is an ever-present peril for readers. Other poems echo less positive themes and subjects Bunyan had previously explored in his literary works. One called 'Upon over-much Niceness', accompanied by a woodcut of a woman in a low-cut formal dress, holding a fan and gazing at herself in a mirror, condemns those who attend to their physical and outward appearance while neglecting their inner, or spiritual, condition. Here the illustration and the vehemence of the verse – 'Their Bodies they must have trick'd up, and trim,/Their inside full of Filth up to the brim' (*MW VI* 210) recall his passionate denunciations of immorality and worldliness in the privileged classes and particularly in women of rank. The theme is developed in 'Upon Apparel', a four-line poem that announces:

> God gave us Cloaths to hide our *Nakedness*,
> And we by *them*, do *it* expose to View.
> Our Pride, and unclean Minds, *to an excess*,
> By our Apparel we to others shew.

> (*MW VI* 213–4)

This verse is also preceded by an illustration, again of a woman in a dress designed to expose her breasts, which are detailed as finely as woodcut will allow. These poems and their illustrations are reminders of the gulf between attitudes to the body in the fashionable world of the Restoration period and of the Nonconformist community. A modern reader may be a little surprised to find the images, which appear quite early in the book, in *A Book for Boys and Girls* and, while we should not assume that seventeenth-century children would be shielded from such material, it is likely that they were designed to address a different, adult, group of readers.

A Book for Boys and Girls is explicitly addressed not only to children but to adults who have failed to understand the message of salvation when it was presented to them in other forms. Bunyan's understanding of the effectiveness of allowing his readers to learn through recognizing the ordinary, everyday world around them informed his earlier, allegorical and literary works but here he is delivering his message in his most accessible form, in poems that are entertaining and instructive.

In common with most of Bunyan's literary or narrative texts, this has a preface that rewards close attention almost as much as the main body, especially for those who are interested in how Bunyan viewed his role as a writer and in the changing relationships between writing and faith in seventeenth-century society. Here, Bunyan describes his twin aims, of encouraging literacy and engaging readers who include not only children but adults for whom the material provided by other writers has proved unappealing, or ineffective. In the opening lines of his prefatory verse he describes the *'proper Subjects of this Book'*: *'Boys and Girls of all Sorts and Degrees,/ From those of Age, to Children on the Knees'*. To reinforce the scope of his definition of the *'childish'*, he continues: *'We now have Boys with Beards, and Girls that be/ Big as old Women, wanting Gravity'* (*MW VI* 190). These adults are seen, in a phrase that brings to mind the world of Restoration drama, as preoccupied with *'all the frantic Fopp'ries of this Age'* and as indifferent to the messages of ministers who had addressed them as men and women. To reach these damnably immature adults Bunyan will *'like a Fool stand fing'ring of their toys;/ And all to shew them, they are Girls and Boys'* (*MW VI* 191). After his lengthy consideration of these potential readers, their

75

vices and limitations, it is easy to see why the subject of improper dress, complete with vivid images, might be found a few pages later.

Bunyan, as always, is careful to show that there is scriptural precedent for his literary methods, citing the example of Solomon's use of the ant in his teaching, and also anticipates the derision with which the educated may respond to his deliberately simple rhymes, noting that if he has any success '*I have my end, tho I my self expose/ To scorn; God will have Glory in the close*' (*MW VI* 192). It is a clear and passionate declaration of his purpose: to use everyday '*Toys*' to convey God's message. The preface then turns, briefly, to actual children and announces that he intends to teach them '*what the Letters be,/ And how they may improve their* A, B, C', reminding '*my pretty Children*' that '*All must there begin, that wou'd be wise*' (*MW VI* 192). The preface is duly followed by a spelling guide that is designed to help its readers embark on the first steps to reading. This links Bunyan to the Nonconformist tradition of encouraging literacy as the foundation of individual reading of Scripture as a vital part of the redemptive process and the spelling guide is presented as 'enough for little Children to prepare themselves for Psalter, or Bible' (*MW VI* 196). So the book that offers examples of divine meaning in the book of nature will also help people read God's word in print.

The spelling guide itself, however, makes no reference to meaning, only to how words are constructed in a systematic fashion according to numbers of letters, vowels and consonants. Words of different lengths are presented in a table, marked with syllable breaks, and a list of non-words that do not conform to these structural rules is offered: 'sl, gld, strnght, spll, drll, fll' (*MW VI* 194). It is intriguing to see this example of what might be called structural linguistics in a late work by this most devout of authors. Bunyan regularly signalled his anxiety that the process of communicating God's truth in written form was fraught with dangers of misinterpretation and he repeatedly reminded his readers not to be distracted by the superficial aspects of texts. Here, though, he presents a model of language in which words are learned without reference to meaning, divine or other, and while this in no way indicates any change in his position it does anticipate what will later become a dominant secular model. One other aspect of this spelling guide may also intrigue a modern reader who is used to noting the multiple, and sometimes competing, meanings of a text. Bunyan's list of three-letter words is as follows: 'But, for, her, she, did, doe, all, his, way, you, may, say, nay' (*MW VI* 194). The words are presented like preceding lists but unlike them, if this list is read from start to end, it appears, despite the commas, to work as a meaningful phrase: but for her she did do all his way you may say nay. There are no indications that this was a deliberate phrase but it does resonate in the context of Bunyan's positive and challenging relationships with, and representations of, women. We could, as modern readers, apply it to Christiana, or Agnes Beaumont, or Sister Witt. In short, it acts as a reminder that it is in the process of interpreting that readers release the meaning of texts and this anticipates the next phase of Bunyan's literary contribution as his writings circulate after his death.

Bunyan's prefatory material, including the spelling guide, were omitted, with a selection of poems, from popular editions after his death, and the intriguing scope, and vulnerability, of Bunyan's ambition for his last literary work was contained by editorial intervention. Yet, as studies from a variety of perspectives have shown, his writings, and especially *The Pilgrim's Progress* would, in the coming centuries, prove remarkably resilient as generations of editors and publishers sought to harness them to different causes across the world.

In the years after *The Pilgrim's Progress: The Second Part* and up to his death in 1688, Bunyan continued to pursue his pastoral ministry, both through writing, and in preaching and meetings in his own county and beyond. He died, perhaps fittingly, while engaged in pastoral work, becoming gravely ill after an exhausting journey to intercede in a family dispute. His death came just months before the 'Glorious Revolution' saw the enthroning of the Protestant monarchs William and Mary and the Declaration of Rights and Toleration Acts that, albeit in limited fashion, marked the end of the active persecution of Nonconformists.

It seems poignant that Bunyan, who had lived through revolutionary hopes and traumas, and the long years of persecution and disappointment that ensued, should die just before this moment. Yet from a perspective that recognizes his utter commitment to the greater reality and value of a world to come, we should perhaps be wary of placing too great an emphasis on the impact of the restoration of the Protestant establishment. Bunyan had trodden a difficult path between implied criticism of an antichristian establishment of his day, contrasted with past monarchs who had championed divine truth, and rejection of the potential lawlessness and amorality of the antinomians we might call Protestant extremists. He was, in many senses, both traditionalist and conservative in social matters, but was, by virtue of his faith, set on the straight and narrow path to confrontation with those who placed observance of man's law above observance of God's. While life for Bunyan after the 'Glorious Revolution' might have been less fraught with dangers, it would have surely never have been comfortable. Bunyan may have died in 1688 but his texts have had a rich and varied afterlife. In the life of his written legacy, and particularly of *The Pilgrim's Progress*, after his death, we can see how the texts of this seventeenth-century Nonconformist have continued to unsettle, encourage, and inspire readers in very different social and cultural contexts.

9

Bunyan in the World

A Book for Boys and Girls can be read as Bunyan's attempt to promote the Christian message to an ever-wider group of readers by addressing those for whom literacy is a new experience. This was a logical extension of the reach of *The Pilgrim's Progress* which, even in the author's lifetime, had been what would today be called an international bestseller. Although Bunyan mentioned this in the preface to the second part of the allegory, the book's success was, in his own terms, to be judged not on sales, or on critical acclaim, but on pastoral or religious impact. To Bunyan, writing was an attempt to encourage men, women, and later, children, to recognize and play their parts as sinners seeking salvation within a Christian discourse that alone created meaning in and the meaning of, their lives.

While some Christian scholars may see this as still the greatest value of his work, Bunyan's writings, like all texts, have a history that differs from their author's expectations. This final chapter cannot offer an exhaustive survey but it will indicate the diverse contexts, receptions and interpretation of Bunyan's writings from his death to the current day.

BUNYAN AT HOME

There is perhaps an irony in the title of Bunyan's *A Book for Boys and Girls* as a successor to *The Pilgrim's Progress* in his 'literary' rather than doctrinal writings. In the Britain of the 1960s, when I first encountered the most famous allegory of Western literature, it was as a Sunday school prize. While, as I would later discover, the work was given serious, if somewhat marginal attention, in the university-taught canon of great English literature, its popular readership in Bunyan's native land had dwindled, and its perceived appeal appeared diminished, to the point that it was a respectable award for diligent children in an also diminishing Christian tradition.

The Pilgrim's Progress had, by then, already had an illustrious history as a suitable, edifying book for children as studies of its appearance in, and influence on, classic tales of childhood attest; from Louisa May Alcott and Mark Twain to Enid Blyton, influential writers for children acknowledged the impact of Bunyan's allegory as a nursery library staple.[1] But if Bunyan's allegory had held a place in the nursery or children's bookshelf consistently until the mid-twentieth century, his standing in the various canons and markets of adult literature has been less assured.

Bunyan's works were first collected and published together in a folio edition by one of his publishers and friends, Charles Doe, in 1692. Bunyan's worth had been noted before in some prefaces and comments on individual works but it is this folio, and Doe's afterword 'The Struggler', that is generally accepted as signalling the recognition of Bunyan's theological importance as a writer.[2] The folio was advertised in advance and produced, as was customary, by subscription and included an engraved portrait of the author, eulogies by ministers, and Doe's account of Bunyan's struggles. It includes twenty-two treatises and theological works, some published for the first time, and deserves its place as the first collected works. Modern readers might be surprised to learn that this folio did not include the 'literary' works that might seem now to be his greatest achievement but, as Bunyan scholars have noted, the folio was designed to preserve and disseminate Bunyan's writings, for use in church and home. As these had initially been printed as pamphlets they might soon have been lost. Already printed in book form, a work like *The Pilgrim's Progress*, was assured of greater physical longevity and had, as Bunyan knew, spread his name as well as his message far and wide.

Doe's folio began the process of establishing a definitive catalogue of this prolific writer's work. The lengthy history of the efforts to work out exactly what and when Bunyan wrote would take too much space for this volume, but the study of his relationships with printers and booksellers in the dynamic and dangerous world of seventeenth-century publishing has been productive both for Bunyan scholars and for literary and cultural historians. Key editions after Bunyan's death and before the now-definitive Clarendon Press editions included the book-collector George Offor's three-volume *Works of John Bunyan*, published in 1860, that became the standard for the many popular editions of Bunyan's works that were found in chapels and homes.[3] A search of current editions of Bunyan's writings reveals that his works are still produced by religious publishers across the world, especially in North America, and it is possible to argue that while Bunyan's *literary* reception has been subject to changing fashions and priorities, as a Christian author, he has consistently been adopted, adapted, and promoted within evangelical publishing. The second section of this chapter will explore some of this history but first it is worth considering the history of Bunyan's writings and his own place at home.

The value and standing of Bunyan's writing, judged in religious terms, is closely tied to the history of Nonconformist Christianity as it develops through the eighteenth and nine-teenth centuries into Baptist, dissenting, Methodist and 'low-church' Anglican traditions. While there have always been Roman Catholics and 'high-church' Anglicans who have recognized the importance of Bunyan's work, it is the inheritors of his Nonconformist model of Christianity, including but by no means exclusively Calvinists, who have been most influential in shaping the popular religious 'image' of Bunyan as a man whose humble origins and vigorous rather than 'elevated' style, in life and writing, added to his pastoral worth. Such publishers, and readers, sustained Bunyan's reputation through periods when these same qualities were judged by the literary elite to make his writing at best a homespun curiosity; a fair analogy might be with some art critics' views of naive painting.

Bunyan's writings clearly found little favour among the eighteenth-century champions of the Augustan and polite traditions but his best-known text was allotted an honourable, if marginal, place in the developing, and as yet informal, literary canon: Samuel Johnson voiced the key aspects of Bunyan's work that were deemed to mitigate his crudeness of language, tone, and form, when he reportedly praised the inventiveness, imagination and story of *The Pilgrim's Progress*.[4] These attributes would bring Bunyan back to wider favour as the Romantics challenged the orthodoxies of their predecessors and prioritized the work of imagination. Robert Southey, poet laureate, produced an edition of *The Pilgrim's Progress* with a prefatory essay that explored Bunyan's skill as an allegorist; William Blake, a Nonconformist, provided illustrations for another edition of *The Pilgrim's Progress*.

The Romantic writer and critic Samuel Taylor Coleridge coined, in a note he wrote when reading the same text, an opposition that has continued to figure (not always helpfully) in literary discussion of Bunyan. Coleridge wrote that in *The Pilgrim's Progress* 'the Bunyan of Parnassus had the better of the Bunyan of the Conventicle'.[5] This assumed opposition between literary inspiration and religious commitment is not one Bunyan would have recognized, nor is it one that many modern literary critics who emphasize the role that social and cultural conditions, relationships, and discourses have on textual production and reception would find useful. This opposition is best viewed not as a founding tension in the consciousness of the author, John Bunyan, for whom divine inspiration and commitment to writing as an extension of pastoral ministry, were co-requisites of his mission, but as pointing to one of the tensions in the founding of a discipline: English literature. Through the nineteenth and twentieth centuries, as the study of English literature was established as a respectable alternative to the ancient classics, the terms by which literary merit would be judged would be debated and renegotiated, but it is possible to argue that when the value of the study of literature *per se* had to be defended, the need to stress the importance of those *literary* characteristics as *opposed* to those from other fields, such as theology or history, was paramount. To claim that Bunyan's creative inspiration, from Parnassus, home of the muses, overrode his commitment to the religious culture of his own moment co-opts him for a vision of literature as timeless and universal.

Bunyan was not, however, one of the authors given the most attention in the nascent discipline. In 1928 the tercentenary of Bunyan's birth was celebrated with a surge of publications including new biographies, critical and popular studies and newspaper articles. But while *The Pilgrim's Progress* was still singled out for praise, in the *Times Literary Supplement* Edmund Blunden noted the absence of a critical edition of Bunyan's works and elsewhere James Rendel Harris called for the 'methods of higher criticism' to be applied to Bunyan's writings.[6]

Although Bunyan was still a relatively marginal figure in the literary canon when I was an undergraduate, many methods of literary and cultural criticism have been applied to him since 1928. In traditional literary criticism topics included Bunyan's influence on the development of the allegory and contribution to the early novel form. However Bunyan has always attracted the attention of those for whom a purely formal literary criticism has seemed inadequate or inapposite. The tercentenary of Bunyan's death in 1988 was given far less coverage in the popular press, but academic and scholarly publications revealed a burgeoning serious interest. Two figures – it is impossible to include more – whose dedicated work on Bunyan cannot be overestimated include Roger Sharrock, who initiated and oversaw the indispensible multi-volume Clarendon Press *Miscellaneous Works*. Sharrock epitomized the fusion of literary and historical attention that has characterized Bunyan studies since, and helped to bring a new generation of academics to the subject, together with the historian Richard Greaves, whose meticulous work on the seventeenth-century Nonconformity has allowed Bunyan to be placed within a complex socio-cultural and religious network.

By the early twenty-first century, it would be fair to say that with an energetic scholars' network, The International John Bunyan Society, with well-attended conferences, and a dedicated academic journal, *Bunyan Studies*, the study of his work is more extensive and varied than it has ever been. This may reflect, in part, the enduring appeal of his work in literary or religious terms that might have been shared by the Romantics or the Nonconformists. A significant number of scholars approach Bunyan from a position of faith and might be argued, as one literary critic has, to be nearer to Bunyan's own model of reading and interpreting his work than others.[7] The current health of Bunyan studies, however, must also be recognized as fed by a very different tradition.

Bunyan's working-class origins and his repeated criticisms of the wealthy ungodly, combined with the message of a life beyond the oppressions and miseries of daily life, have often appealed to those looking for a new life in this world rather than, like Bunyan, after death. The history of the role played by Bunyan's texts in the popular and political movements that often saw their origins in, or shared members with, radical and Nonconformist religious groups, was recorded, and celebrated, by influential British Marxist scholars including Jack Lindsay, Alick West, Arnold Kettle and Christopher Hill. Reading each of these successive studies, both historical and literary, reveals the changing priorities and methods of Marxist approaches to texts and contexts.[8] Marxist critics approached Bunyan from two main angles: as a facet of the long history of working-class culture and as a part of one of, if not the, key eras of political change, the mid-seventeenth century, or the English Revolution. E. P. Thompson's influential *The Making of the English Working Class* asserted that *The Pilgrim's Progress* was, with Thomas Paine's *Rights of Man*, 'one of the two foundation texts of the English working-class movement'.[9] The comment was fair, reflecting the book's evident popularity in the successive generations who constituted the working-class movement in its various forms, and the vital role played by Nonconformist and Dissenting religion in socio-political activism. The place of religion, and religious belief, in radical movements was not always recognized or given full weight in Marxist analyses which tended to see it as a precursor of secular revolutionary consciousness. The second approach to Bunyan, locating him within the radical social context of the seventeenth-century helped to uncover a complex world in which religious groups and texts could not be neatly understood in a secular framework. The productive and far-reaching intellectual legacy of this tradition was largely endowed by one man.

Christopher Hill's *A Turbulent, Seditious, and Factious People: John Bunyan and his Church* was one of the texts published in the tercentenary of Bunyan's death. As its title proclaims, this study focuses on Bunyan's place both within the political struggles of his day and within a collective, 'his Church'. Hill's lifetime of work on the seventeenth century had turned our understanding of it upside down, revealing the tumult of radical ideas and groupings that fed the English Revolution, and his approach to Bunyan situated his work in relation to that context. Hill's work has been extremely influential, particularly in British historical approaches, although many of his academic successors do not share his Marxist commitment to revolutionary change and greater emphasis on the role of more radical political sects. But it is a final chapter in his 1988 study that signals the most significant journey taken by Bunyan's writing, one which took his texts not into the study of the academic or the university library, but into the mission schools, and hands of readers across the world.

In his final chapter Hill notes that *The Pilgrim's Progress* is no longer a bestseller in his native land and he briefly anticipates an aspect of Bunyan studies that has recently come to the fore: the story of Bunyan 'abroad'.

BUNYAN ABROAD

The history of the global travels of Bunyan's writings has much to reveal about the interaction of texts and societies. In the preface to *The Pilgrim's Progress: The Second Part*, Bunyan lists the countries in which the earlier book has been well received – France, Flanders, Holland – and counts 'Highlanders, *and* Wild-Irish' among its readers (*PP II* 161) and it is easy to imagine the impact and popularity of the work in the context of European Protestantism where the author would surely be preaching to the converted. Although he notes the international reach of his book as significant, in his comments on his aims as a writer, Bunyan concentrates on having an impact on readers who have missed the message of salvation at home, focusing on reaching different ages, genders, and social classes. It is tempting, however, to see in the reference to the highlanders and 'wild' Irish, neither of whom fits in the assumed protestant community, hints at the possible use of the text in conversion abroad. The history of its translation, publication, and dissemination in the coming centuries shows clearly that it has been one of the most popular aids to communicating the message of Christianity, for its own sake, and tied in to other discourses up to the present day. But just as we cannot know precisely how the highlanders and Irish readers responded to *The Pilgrim's Progress*, so we must be wary of assuming that the history of Bunyan's writing outside his native land is one of passive reception. Bunyan's writings have, as the critic Isabel Hofmeyer has trenchantly argued, a 'transnational' history, that exceeds, and is too often occluded by, his reputation as an 'English' writer and it seems fitting that this study ends with a glimpse of that world.[10]

While Bunyan's standing in literary, as opposed to religious, terms has been subject to the changing social and cultural contexts that underpin agreed ideas of what constitutes great or accomplished writing, *The Pilgrim's Progress* has appeared to march onwards and outwards from the Bedford gaol into ever-more-varied spaces of reading across the globe. *The Pilgrim's Progress* was translated into an ever-increasing number of languages from its publication.[11] Some were literary editions but a majority were produced as part of the missionary activity that was concurrent with, and had an uneasy relationship with, the imperial and colonial drives of Britain, other European nations and the United States. Nonconformist evangelists and later Protestant missionary movements funded translations and editions of the book wherever they operated and at times of energetic colonial activity: the publication of numerous editions in various African languages coincides with British imperial expansion in the continent in the mid-nineteenth and early-twentieth centuries, while translation into Cree, Dakota, and Cheyenne coincides with the United States' government's attempts to control and westernize the native American nations.[12] Translations were often accompanied by teaching aids, like spelling guides, and useful local information. Many editions explicitly sought to appeal to target readerships, with illustrations that emphasized the links between their world and that of the text, such as a Canton version in 1870 that featured 'Chinese illustrations' of key scenes in the allegory.[13]

Approaches to understanding the ways in which translated editions of Bunyan's work have functioned have changed considerably in recent years. In 1928 the critic Augustine Birrell described Bunyan as 'a plain Englishman to the core, and as good an Imperialist as it is possible for any Christian man to be'[14] and the translations of *The Pilgrim's Progress* were undoubtedly used within imperialist and colonialist drives to enlist non-Western, non-Christian subjects to the values succinctly described by the explorer and missionary David Livingstone as 'Christianity, Commerce, and Civilisation'.[15] The international reach of *The Pilgrim's Progress* undoubtedly contributed to Bunyan's standing as an important figure of English literature, as the lives of literary texts outside their first context always do but the history of even this evangelical text is complex and hard to reduce to a neat narrative. It is, of course, unfair to associate Bunyan with attempts to harness his message to later political strategies and the Christianity promoted by translated editions is usually a different one to the author's. Nevertheless, the explicit use of *The Pilgrim's Progress* to convert reveals how valuable the allegory was thought to be.

Livingstone's letters reveal much about missionary conversion techniques and how a text like *The Pilgrim's Progress* could seem an ideal tool. He wrote to family and friends of his attempts to convert a chief from Bechuanaland (Botswana) called Sechele: starting by teaching him to read his own language using spelling guides that echo Bunyan's in *A Book for Boys and Girls* and culminating in him reading a translation of *The Pilgrim's Progress* by Livingstone's father-in-law Robert Moffat. Livingstone was elated by the fact that Sechele's response to the story of Christian – 'Some parts of the Pilgrim's experience and his are exactly alike, and makes him extol the wisdom of Johane Bunyana'[16] – had helped him overcome his initial resistance to giving up what Livingstone, dismissive of cultural difference, called his *superfluous* wives. In Livingstone's account Sechele had, like Christian, fought his own, and his people's, resistance to the sacrifices and struggles needed to follow the path to salvation. The combination of text, translator and missionary guiding the reader had kept him on the straight and narrow path. Sadly, for Livingstone at least, a few months later he reports that Sechele had resumed sexual relations with more than one wife and had, despite expressing contrition, been suspended from communion and expelled from fellowship; soon after this Livingstone suggests some revisions to Moffat's translation (which used the wrong dialect for some words) and left Bechuanaland, denouncing the locals as 'truly *slow* of heart to believe'.[17] Livingstone moved on to other parts of Africa and made his name as an explorer, while still seeing his mission as Christian; Sechele continued to rule until his death in 1892 and there is no evidence he returned to the Christian fold.

This is, of course, only one story of *The Pilgrim's Progress* in Africa, told from the perspective of the disappointed Western missionary. In *The Portable Bunyan: A Transnational History of The Pilgrim's Progress* Isabel Hofmeyer explores many aspects of the complex history of *The Pilgrim's Progress* in Africa that moves beyond the model of Western missionary and African convert/ resister, tracing ways in which the text was remade by its African translators and readers and the impact this had on its status.[18]

One of the key reasons for *The Pilgrim's Progress*'s enduring appeal to diverse readers in cultural and historical moments so very different to Bunyan's is clearly the theme of a troubled man struggling to defeat internal and external forces to reach a better life. Christopher Hill told the story of the Taiping rebellion in mid-nineteenth-century China when the radical Christian sect nearly overcame the combined forces of the state and its imperial allies. He noted that the leader, Hong Xiuquan, had two favourite books, the Bible and *The Pilgrim's Progress*, and noted that if the Taiping had won 'Bunyan's allegory might have become China's earlier little red book'.[19] Hill's point deftly signals the complex ways in which readers transform texts but he does not note that the commander of the British force sent to fight the Taiping, General Charles George Gordon, was later to describe his own involvement in military campaigns in terms derived from the same allegory.[20] Perhaps neither Hong Xiuquan nor Gordon would have been reading the story of Christian in a way that might have satisfied Bunyan. Did they pay too much attention to the 'outside', as he warned readers might? Did they ignore, or even have, his 'key', his marginal notes and pointing fingers to show them how to interpret his words?

Bunyan's readers, from those he envisaged in his lifetime, to those who read his work in Braille, in Turkish, or now online, encounter and interpret texts that are neither singular nor static. They are emphatic, pointing readers along a narrow, tricky path to what the author hopes may be their salvation. They are dogmatic, written in the service of a truth that their author believed fervently to define humankind's place and possibilities in a created world. They are written through with the values and priorities of their time and place. But they are also moving, uplifting, provocative texts that have helped to shape many different communities of readers across the world and so have histories that will continue to be written beyond the page.

Notes

CHAPTER 1. INTRODUCTION

1. For a summary of sociological approaches to the religious and challenges to secularization theory, see Stephen Hunt, *Religion and Everyday Life* (Abingdon: Routledge, 2005).
2. Stuart Sim, 'Bunyan and his Fundamentalist Readers', in W. R. Owens and Stuart Sim (eds.), *Reception, Appropriation, Recollection: Bunyan's' Pilgrim's Progress', Religions and Discourse 33* (Bern: Peter Lang, 2007), 225.

CHAPTER 2. BUNYAN'S WORLD

1. Stachniewski, John, 'Introduction', John Bunyan, *Grace Abounding with other spiritual autobiographies* (Oxford: Oxford University Press), xv–xviii.
2. For a useful analysis of the evidence, and of alternative interpretations, see Anne Laurence, 'Bunyan and the Parliamentary Army', in Anne Laurence, W. R. Owens and Stuart Sim, *John Bunyan and his England, 1628–88* (London: Hambledon, 1990), 17–29.
3. The phrase, originally in Acts 17.6, and used in a 1640s pamphlet, was adopted as the title of one of the most influential studies of the period, Christopher Hill, *The World Turned Upside Down* (Harmondsworth: Penguin, 1975).

CHAPTER 3. BUNYAN AS PREACHER: EARLY WRITING AND *GRACE ABOUNDING TO THE CHIEF OF SINNERS*

1. 'A Relation of the Imprisonment of Mr. John Bunyan', *Grace Abounding*, 106.
2. 'A Relation of the Imprisonment of Mr. John Bunyan', *Grace*

Abounding, 116–20; for a fuller consideration of Bunyan's views on women see Chapter 7.

3. See N. H. Keeble, *The Literary Culture of Nonconformity in Later Seventeenth-Century England* (Leicester: Leicester University Press, 1987).

4. Bunyan, John, *The Miscellaneous Works of John Bunyan, Volume I*, ed. T. L. Underwood (Oxford: Clarendon Press, 1980), 139.

5. See especially Davies, Michael, *Graceful Reading: Theology and Narrative in the Works of John Bunyan* (Oxford: Oxford University Press, 2002).

6. Frontispiece of *Christian Behaviour* reprinted in Bunyan, John, *The Miscellaneous Works of John Bunyan, Volume III*, ed. J. Sears McGee (Oxford: Clarendon Press, 1987), 8.

CHAPTER 4. BUNYAN AS WRITER: *THE PILGRIM'S PROGRESS*

1. George Whalley (ed.), *The Collected Works of Samuel Taylor Coleridge: Marginalia I* (London: Routledge, 1980), 801.

2. N. H. Keeble, 'Introduction', John Bunyan, *The Pilgrim's Progress* (Oxford: Oxford University Press, 1984), xii–xiii.

3. W. R. Owens, 'Note on the Text', John Bunyan, *The Pilgrim's Progress* (Oxford: Oxford University Press, 2003), xxxix.

4. For a full discussion of Latitudinarianism, see Isabel Rivers, *Reason, Grace, and Sentiment: A Study of the Language of Religion and Ethics in England 1660–1780, Volume I Whichcote to Wesley* (Cambridge: Cambridge University Press, 1991).

5. N. H. Keeble, 'Introduction', John Bunyan, *The Pilgrim's Progress*, xvii.

6. John Foxe, *Acts and Monuments of Matters most Special and Memorable, Happening in the Church, with an Universall Historie of the Same*, 3 vols.

7. Arnold Kettle, cited in Christopher Hill, *A Turbulent, Seditious, and Factious People: John Bunyan and His Church*, 206.

8. See Tamsin Spargo, 'Bunyans Abounding, or the Names of the Author', in N. H. Keeble (ed.), *John Bunyan: Reading Dissenting Writing*, 79–101 for an exploration of the changing ways in which Bunyan was presented as a writer in editions of his works.

CHAPTER 5. *THE LIFE AND DEATH OF MR BADMAN*

1. See Stuart Sim, 'Bunyan and early novel: *The Life and Death of Mr Badman*', Anne Dunan-Page (ed.), *The Cambridge Companion to Bunyan* (Cambridge: Cambridge University Press, 2010), 95–106.

2. See James F. Forrest and Roger Sharrock, 'Introduction', *The Life and Death of Mr Badman*, xiii–xv.
3. See David Hawkes, 'Master of His Ways? Determinism and the Market in *The Life and Death of Mr. Badman*', in N. H. Keeble (ed.), *John Bunyan: Reading Dissenting Writing* (Oxford: Peter Lang, 2002), 211–30.
4. See Roger Pooley, 'The Life and Death of Mr. Badman and Seventeenth-Century Discourses of Atheism', in N. H. Keeble (ed.), *John Bunyan: Reading Dissenting Writing*, 199–210.

CHAPTER 6. *THE HOLY WAR*

1. Roger Sharrock and James F. Forrest, 'Introduction', *John Bunyan, The Holy War* (Oxford: Oxford University Press, 1980), xxxv.
2. Arlette Zinck, 'From Apocalypse to Prophecy: the Didactic Strategies of *The Holy War*', in N. H. Keeble (ed.), *John Bunyan: Reading Dissenting Writing*, 183–98.
3. Roger Sharrock, *John Bunyan*, 118.
4. Examples can be found in the writings of St Paul, Langland and Spenser as well as in popular miracle and mystery plays of the Middle Ages.
5. Bunyan, *Israel's Hope Encouraged* (Offor, i, 585), quoted in Roger Sharrock and James F. Forrest, 'Introduction', *John Bunyan, The Holy War*, xxi.
6. Christopher Hill, *A Turbulent, Seditious, and Factious People*, 240.
7. David Walker, 'Militant Religion and Politics in *The Holy War*', in Anne Dunan-Page, *The Cambridge Companion to Bunyan* (Cambridge: Cambridge University Press, 2010), 109.
8. Richard Greaves, *Glimpses of Glory*, 417.
9. For contrasting views see Stuart Sim and David Walker, *Bunyan and Authority: The Rhetoric of Dissent and the Legitimation Crisis in Seventeenth-Century England* (Bern: Peter Lang, 2000), 213 and Daniel V. Runyon, '*The Holy War*: Sanctification as Spiritual Warfare', *Bunyan Studies 12* (2006/2007), 105–17.
10. See Beth Lynch, '"Rather Dark to Readers in General": Some Critical Casualties of John Bunyan's *The Holy War* (1682)', *Bunyan Studies 9* (1999/2000), 25–49.

CHAPTER 7. *THE PILGRIM'S PROGRESS: THE SECOND PART*

1. N. H. Keeble, 'Introduction', *The Pilgrim's Progress*, xviii.
2. Christopher Hill, *A Turbulent, Seditious and Factious People*, 299.

3. Tamsin Spargo, *The Writing of John Bunyan*, 83–95.
4. See Vera Camden (ed.), *The Narrative of the Persecutions of Agnes Beaumont* (East Lansing: Colleagues, 1992). The text is also included in John Stachniewski (ed.), *Grace Abounding* with *Other Spiritual Autobiographies* (Oxford: Oxford World's Classics, 1998), 191–224.

CHAPTER 8. *A BOOK FOR BOYS AND GIRLS*

1. Shannon Murray, '*A Book for Boys and Girls, or, Country Rhimes for Children*: Bunyan and Literature for Children', in Anne Dunan-Page (ed.), *The Cambridge Companion to Bunyan* (Cambridge: Cambridge University Press), 120.
2. The most popular English emblem books were George Withers, *Collection of Emblems, Ancient and Moderne* (1625) and Francis Quarles, *Emblems Divine and Moral* (1635).

CHAPTER 9. BUNYAN IN THE WORLD

1. See Shannon Murray, '*A Book for Boys and Girls*' in Anne Dunan-Page (ed.), *The Cambridge Companion to Bunyan* (Cambridge: Cambridge University Press), 120.
2. See W. R. Owens, 'Reading the Bibliographical Codes: Bunyan's Publication in Folio', in N. H. Keeble, *John Bunyan: Reading Dissenting Writing*, 59–77.
3. George Offor (ed.), *The Works of John Bunyan* (Glasgow and Edinburgh: Blackie and Son).
4. R. W. Chapman (ed.), *Boswell's Life of Johnson* (Evanston, Ill.: Northwestern University Press, 1974), 529.
5. George Whalley (ed.), *The Collected Work of Samuel Taylor Coleridge: Marginalia I* (London: Routledge and Kegan Paul, 1980), 801.
6. See James F. Forrest and Richard L. Greaves, *John Bunyan: A Reference Guide* (Boston: G. K. Hall, 1982), 203–26.
7. See Michael Davis, *Graceful Reading*.
8. See David Herreshoff, 'Marxist Perspectives on Bunyan', in Robert G. Collmer (ed.), *Bunyan in Our Time* (Kent, Ohio: Kent State University Press, 1989), 161–85.
9. E. P. Thompson, *The Making of the English Working Class* (Harmondsworth: Penguin, 1968), 34.
10. Isabel Hofmeyer, *The Portable Bunyan: A Transnational History of The Pilgrim's Progress* (Princeton: Princeton University, 2004).
11. See Spargo, *The Writing of John Bunyan*, 104–5 for a survey from seventeenth- to early-twentieth century translations.

12. Cree (1886), Dakota (1857) and Cheyenne (1904) and see Peter N. Carroll and David W. Noble, *The Free and the Unfree: a New History of the United States* (Harmondsworth: Penguin, 1988), 165–84.
13. Rev. G. Piercy (trans.), *The Pilgrim's Progress* (Wesleyan Mission, 1870).
14. Augustine Birrell, 'Links of Empire-books (IX): *The Pilgrim's Progress*', *Empire Review* 47 (February 1928), 79–87, quoted in Richard L. Greaves, 'Bunyan through the centuries: some reflections', *English Studies* 64 (1983), 119.
15. Quoted in Thomas Packenham, *The Scramble for Africa* (London: Abacus, 1991), xxiv.
16. I. Schapera (ed.), *David Livingstone: Family Letters 1841–1856, Volume II* (London: Chatto and Windus, 1993), 19.
17. Schapera (ed.), *David Livingstone; Family Letters 1841–1856, Volume I*, 15.
18. Isabel Hofmeyer, *The Portable Bunyan: A Transnational History of The Pilgrim's Progress* (Princeton: Princeton University, 2004).
19. Hill, *A Turbulent, Seditious, and Factious People*, 375.
20. Packenham, *The Scramble for Africa*, 82.

Select Bibliography

WRITINGS BY JOHN BUNYAN

Bunyan's Works

Bunyan's writings are listed in order of first publication. The standard scholarly source of individual works is given in parenthesis. ? denotes probable date.

Some Gospel-Truths Opened	1656 (*MW I*)
A Vindiction of Some Gospel-Truths Opened	1657 (*MW I*)
A Few Sighs from Hell	1658 (*MW I*)
The Doctrine of the Law and Grace Unfolded	1659 (*MW II*)
Profitable Meditations	1661 (*MW VI: Poems*)
I Will Pray with the Spirit	1662 (*MW II*)
Prison Meditations	1663 (*MW VI: Poems*)
Christian Behaviour	1663 (*MW II*)
A Map, shewing the order and causes of Salvation and Damnation	1663? (*MW XII*)
One thing is needful	1665 (*MW VI: Poems*)
Ebal and Gerizzim	1665 (*MW VI: Poems*)
The Holy City	1665 (*MW III*)
The Resurrection of the Dead	1665 (*MW III*)
Grace Abounding to the Chief of Sinners	1666
The Heavenly Footman	1671? (*MW V*)
A Defence of the Doctrine of Justification By Faith	1672 (*MW IV*)
A Confession of My Faith and A Reason of My Practice in Worship	1672 (*MW IV*)
Differences in Judgment about Water-Baptism	
No Bar to Communion	1673 (*MW IV*)
The Barren Fig-tree	1673 (*MW IV*)
Peaceable Principles and True	1674 (*MW V*)

Light for them that sit in Darkness	1675 (*MW VIII*)
Instruction for the Ignorant	1675 (*MW VIII*)
Saved by Grace	1676 (*MW VIII*)
The Strait Gate	1676 (*MW V*)
Come, and Welcome, to Jesus Christ	1678 (*MW VIII*)
The Pilgrim's Progress	1678
A Treatise of the Fear of God	1679 (*MW IX*)
The Life and Death of Mr Badman	1680
The Holy War	1682
The Greatness of the Soul	1682 (*MW IX*)
A Case of Conscience Resolved	1683 (*MW IV*)
A Holy Life	1683 (*MW IX*)
Seasonable Counsel, or Advice to Sufferers	1684 (*MW X*)
A Caution to stir up to watch against Sin	1684 (*MW VI: Poems*)
The Pilgrim's Progress: The Second Part	1684
A Discourse upon the Pharisee and the Publicane	1685 (*MW X*)
Questions about the Nature and Perpetuity of the Seventh-Day-Sabbath	1685 (*MW IV*)
A Book for Boys and Girls	1686 (*MW VI: Poems*)
The Advocateship of Jesus Christ	1688 (*MW XI*)
The Jerusalem Sinner Saved, or Good News for the Vilest of Men	1688 (*MW XI*)
A Discussion of the Building, Nature, Excellency and Government of the House of God	1688 (*MW VI: Poems*)
The Water of Life	1688 (*MW VII*)
Solomon's Temple Spiritualized	1688 (*MW VII*)

Works Published Posthumously

Bunyan's Last Sermon	1689 (*MW XII*)
The Acceptable Sacrifice	1689 (*MW XII*)
Justification by an Imputed Righteousness	1692 (*MW XII*)
An Exposition on the Ten First Chapters of Genesis, and Part of the Eleventh	1692 (*MW XII*)
Paul's Departure and Crown	1692 (*MW XII*)
Of the Trinity and a Christian	1692 (*MW XII*)
Of the Law and a Christian	1692 (*MW XII*)
Israel's Hope Encouraged	1692 (*MW XIII*)
The Desire of the Righteous Granted	1692 (*MW XIII*)
The Saints' Privilege and Profit	1692 (*MW XIII*)
Christ a Compleat Saviour	1692 (*MW XIII*)
The Saints' Knowledge of Christ's Love	1692 (*MW XIII*)
Of the House of the Forest of Lebanon	1692 (*MW VII*)

Of Antichrist, and his Ruine	1692 (*MW XIII*)
A Relation of My Imprisonment	1765 (with *Grace Abounding*)

Editions

There are many editions of *Grace Abounding* and *The Pilgrim's Progress*. In the case of these texts, I have chosen to refer to those editions that employ the standard text in paperback format. All other references are to the standard scholarly editions.

Grace Abounding to the Chief of Sinners, eds. John Stachniewski with Anita Pacheco (Oxford, 1998). This edition also includes *The Narrative of the Persecution of Agnes Beaumont* and three other spiritual autobiographies.

The Holy War, eds. R. Sharrock and J. F. Forrest (Oxford, 1980).

The Life and Death of Mr Badman, eds. J. F. Forrest and R. Sharrock (Oxford, 1988).

The Miscellaneous Works of John Bunyan, General Editor, R. Sharrock (Oxford, 1977–94) comprising: *Volume I*, ed. T. L. Underwood (1980); *Volume II*, ed. R. L. Greaves (1976); *Volume III*, ed. J. S. McGee (1986); *Volume IV*, ed. T. L. Underwood (1989); *Volume V*, ed. G. Midgley (1986); *Volume VI (Poems)*, ed. G. Midgley (1980); *Volume VII*, ed. G. Midgley (1989); *Volume VIII*, ed. R. L. Greaves (1979); *Volume IX*, ed. R. L. Greaves (1981); *Volume X*, ed. O. C. Watkins (1988); *Volume XI*, ed. R. L. Greaves (1985); *Volume XII*, ed. W. R. Owens (1994); *Volume XIII*, ed. W. R. Owens (1994).

The Pilgrim's Progress, ed. W. R. Owens (Oxford, 2003).

The Minutes of the First Independent Church (now Bunyan Meeting) at Bedford, 1656–1766, ed. H. G. Tibbutt (Bedford, 1976).

MONOGRAPHS AND COLLECTIONS ON BUNYAN

Batson, E. Beatrice, *John Bunyan: Allegory and Imagination* (London, 1984).

Brown, John, *John Bunyan: His Life, Times and Work* (1885; rev. ed. London, 1928).

Camden, Vera (ed.), *Trauma and Transformation: the Political Progress of John Bunyan* (Stanford, 2007).

Collmer, Robert G. (ed.), *Bunyan In Our Time* (Kent, Ohio, 1989).

Davies, Michael, *Graceful Reading: Theology and Narrative in the Works of John Bunyan* (Oxford, 2002).

de Vries, Pieter, *John Bunyan on the Order of Salvation*, trans. C. van Haaften (New York, 1994).

Dunan-Page, Anne (ed.), *The Cambridge Companion to Bunyan* (Cambridge, 2010).

Forrest, James F. and Richard Greaves, *John Bunyan: A Reference Guide* (Boston, 1982).

Gay, David, James G. Randall and Arlette Zinck (eds.), *Awakening Words: John Bunyan and the Language of Community* (Newark DE and London, 2000).

Greaves, Richard L., *Glimpses of Glory: John Bunyan and English Dissent* (Stanford, 2002).

———, *John Bunyan* (London, 1969).

———, *John Bunyan and English Nonconformity* (London, 1992).

Hancock, Maxine, *The Key in the Window: Marginal Notes in Bunyan's Narratives* (Vancouver, 2000).

Harrison, G. B., *John Bunyan: A Study in Personality* (London, 1928).

Hill, Christopher, *A Turbulent, Seditious, and Factious People: John Bunyan and His Church* (Oxford, 1988).

Hofmeyer, Isabel, *The Portable Bunyan: A Transnational History of the Pilgrims Progress* (Princeton, 2003).

Johnson, Galen, *Prisoner of Conscience: John Bunyan on Self, Community and Christian Faith.*

Johnson, Barbara A., *Reading Piers Plowman and the Pilgrim's Progress: Reception and the Protestant Reader* (Carbondale, Ill., 1992).

Kaufmann, U. Milo, *The Pilgrim's Progress and Puritan Techniques in Meditation* (New Haven, 1966).

Keeble, N. H. (ed.), *John Bunyan: Conventicle and Parnassus – Tercentenary Essays* (Oxford, 1988).

———, (ed.), *John Bunyan: Reading Dissenting Writing* (Bern, 2002).

Laurence, Anne, W. R. Owens and Stuart Sim (eds.), *John Bunyan and his England 1628–88* (London, 1990).

Lindsay, Jack, *John Bunyan: Maker of Myths* (London, 1937).

Newey, Vincent (ed.), *The Pilgrim's Progress: Critical and Historical Views* (Liverpool, 1980).

Owens, W. R. and Stuart Sim (eds.), *Reception, Appropriation, Recollection: Bunyan's 'Pilgrim's Progress', Religions and Discourse 33* (Bern: Peter Lang, 2007).

Runyon, Daniel V., *John Bunyan's Master Story: The Holy War as Battle Allegory in Religious and Biblical Context* (Lampeter: Edwin Mellen, 2007).

Sharrock, Roger, *John Bunyan* (London, 1954; reissued 1968).

———, *John Bunyan: The Pilgrim's Progress* (London: 1966).

———, (ed.), *Bunyan: 'The Pilgrim's Progress': A Casebook* (London, 1976).

Sim, Stuart, *Negotiations with Paradox: Narrative Practice and Narrative Form in Bunyan & Defoe* (London, 1990).

Sim, Stuart and David Walker, *Bunyan and Authority: the Rhetoric of Dissent and the Legitimation Crisis in Seventeenth-Century England* (Bern, 2000).

Spargo, Tamsin, *The Writing of John Bunyan* (Aldershot, 1997).

Swaim, Kathleen M., *Pilgrim's Progress, Puritan Progress: Discourses and Contexts* (Urbana, Ill., 1993).

Talon, Henri, *John Bunyan: The Man and his Works*, trans. Barbara Wall (London, 1951).

Tindall, William Y., *John Bunyan: Mechanick Preacher* (New York, 1934).

Van Os, M. and G. J. Schutte (eds.), *Bunyan in England and Abroad* (Amsterdam, 1990).

Wakefield, Gordon, *John Bunyan: The Christian* (London, 1992; reprinted 1994).

ESSAYS

This list is necessarily selective and the reader is encouraged to consult the journal of the International John Bunyan Society, *Bunyan Studies*, for contemporary articles and reviews.

Breen, Margaret Sonser, 'Christiana's Rudeness: Spiritual Authority in *The Pilgrim's Progress*', *Bunyan Studies* 7 (1997), 96–111.

Camden, Vera J., 'Blasphemy and the Problem of the Self in *Grace Abounding*', *Bunyan Studies* 2 (1989), 5–22.

———, '"Most Fit for a Wounded Conscience": the Place of Luther's "Commentary on Galatians" in *Grace Abounding*', *Renaissance Quarterly*, 50 (1997), 819–49.

Carlton, Peter J., 'Bunyan: Language, Convention, Authority', *English Literary History*, 51 (1984), 108–26.

Dunan, Anne, '*The Life and Death of Mr Badman* as a "Compassionate Counsel to all Young Men": John Bunyan and Nonconformist Writings on Youth', *Bunyan Studies* 9 (1999/2000), 50–68.

Finley, C. Stephen, 'Bunyan among the Victorians', *Literature and Theology* 3: 1 (March 1989), 77–94.

Greaves, Richard, 'Bunyan through the Centuries: Some Reflections', *English Studies* 64 (1983), 113–21.

Johnson, Galen, '"Be Not Extream": The Limits of Theory in Reading John Bunyan', *Christianity and Literature* 49 (2000), 447–64.

Keeble, N. H., 'The Way and the Ways of Puritan Story: Biblical Patterns in Bunyan and his Contemporaries', *English* 33 (1984), 209–32.

Knott, John R., Jr., 'Bunyan and the Holy Community', *Studies in Philology* 80 (1983), 200–25.

Luxon, Thomas H., 'Calvin and Bunyan on Word and Image: Is There a Text in Interpreter's House?', *English Literary Renaissance* 18 (1988), 438–59.

Nussbaum, Felicity A., '"By These Words I Was Sustained": Bunyan's *Grace Abounding'*, *English Literary History* 49 (1982), 18–34.

Pooley, Roger, 'The Structure of *The Pilgrim's Progress'*, *Essays in Poetics*, 4 (1979), 59–70.

Sharrock, Roger, 'Spiritual Autobiography in *The Pilgrim's Progress'*, *Review of English Studies*, 24 (1948), 102–20.

Slights, William W. E., 'Bunyan on the Edge', *Bunyan Studies* 10 (2001/2), 29–45.

Spargo, Tamsin, 'The Purloined Postcard: Waiting for Bunyan', *Textual Practice* 8 (1994), 79–96.

Stranahan, Brainerd P., 'Bunyan's Special Talent: Biblical Texts as "Events" in *Grace Abounding* and *The Pilgrim's Progress'*, *English Literary Renaissance* 11 (1981), 329–43.

Underwood, T. L., '"It pleased me much to contend": John Bunyan as Controversialist', *Church History* 57 (1988), 456–69.

CULTURAL, HISTORICAL AND SOCIAL CONTEXT

Caldwell, Patricia, *The Puritan Conversion Narrative* (Cambridge, 1983).

Cragg, G. R., *Puritanism in the Period of the Great Persecution 1660–1688* (Cambridge, 1957).

Delaney, Paul, *British Autobiography in the Seventeenth Century* (London, 1969).

Ebner, Dean, *Autobiography in Seventeenth-Century England: Theology and Self* (The Hague, 1971).

Greaves, Richard L., *Deliver Us from Evil: The Radical Underground in Britain 1660–1663* (Oxford, 1986).

——, *Enemies under his Feet: Radicals and Nonconformists in Britain, 1664–1667* (Stanford, Calif., 1990).

Haller, William, *The Rise of Puritanism* (London, 1938; reprinted New York, 1957).

Hill, Christopher, *The World Turned Upside Down: Radical Ideas during the English Revolution* (Harmondsworth, 1975).

Keeble, N. H., *The Literary Culture of Nonconformity in Later Seventeenth-Century England* (Leicester, 1987).

——, *Writing of the English Revolution* (Cambridge, 2001).

Knott, John R., *The Sword of the Spirit: Puritan Responses to the Bible* (Chicago, 1980).

Luxon, Thomas, *Literal Figures: Puritan Allegory and the Crisis in Representation* (Chicago, 1995).

McGregor, J. F. and B. Reay, *Radical Religion in the English Revolution* (Oxford, 1984).

Morgan, John, *Godly Learning: Puritan Attitudes towards Reason, Learning and Education, 1560–1640* (Cambridge, 1988).

Nussbaum, Felicity A., *The Autobiographical Subject: Gender and Ideology in Eighteenth-Century England* (Baltimore, 1989).

Rivers, Isabel, *Reason, Grace, and Sentiment: A Study of the Language of Religion and Ethics in England 1660–1780 Volume I: Whichcote to Wesley* (Cambridge, 1991).

Sasek, Lawrence A., *The Literary Temper of the English Puritans* (Baton Rouge, 1961).

Smith, Nigel, *Perfection Proclaimed: Language and Literature in English Radical Religion 1640–1660* (Oxford, 1989).

Stachniewski, John, *The Persecutory Imagination: English Puritanism and the Literature of Religious Despair* (Oxford, 1991).

Thickstun, Margaret Olofson, *Fictions of the Feminine: Puritan Doctrine and the Representation of Women* (Ithaca, NY, 1988).

Van Dyke, Carolyn, *The Fiction of Truth: Structures of Meaning in Narrative and Dramatic Allegory* (Ithaca, NY and London: Cornell University Press, 1985).

Watkins, Owen C., *The Puritan Experience* (London, 1972).

Watts, Michael R., *The Dissenters: from the Reformation to the French Revolution* (Oxford, 1978).

Weber, Max, *The Protestant Ethic and the Spirit of Capitalism* (London, 1978).

Index

Act of Uniformity 11, 21, 30
Allegory 32, 33, 45, 54–6, 57, 62
Antinomianism 19–20

Baptists 12, 19
Bayly, Lewis 10
Beaumont, Agnes 67
Bedford 12, 19, 22, 26, 58, 63
Bible, 26–9, 36–7, 72
Birrell, Augustine 86
Blake, William 82
Bunyan, Elizabeth 18, 66
Bunyan, John:
    Army service 7–9, 57–8
    Arrest and imprisonment
        15–18, 34
    Bedford preaching and
        church leadership 12,
        15–16, 18, 23, 30, 31, 50–1,
        77
    Childhood 6–7
    Death 77
    Family 6–7, 10–12, 16, 18, 66
Works:
    A Book for Boys and Girls 68,
        72–8
    A Case of Conscience Resolved
        64, 65, 66
    A Defence of the Doctrine of
        Justification by Faith 35
    A Treatise of the Fear of God 46

Christian Behaviour 22, 49–50,
    64, 66
Grace Abounding to the Chief of
    Sinners 3, 11, 13, 15–29, 31,
    36
I Will Pray with the Spirit 21
Prison Meditations 22
Profitable Meditations 22
Some Gospel-Truths Opened 19
The Doctrine of the Law and
    Grace Unfolded 20
The Holy City 22
The Holy War 1, 54–60, 61
The Life and Death of Mr
    Badman 4, 47–53, 61, 64
The Pilgrim's Progress 1–2,
    30–46, 47, 70, 71, 73, 78,
    79–80, 86–9
The Pilgrim's Progress: The
    Second Part 61–71, 85–6
Bunyan Studies 83
Burton, John 16

Calvinism 12–14, 19, 25–6
Clarendon Code 21–2, 30
Clarke, Samuel 48
Coleridge, Samuel Taylor 32, 82
Conversion Narratives 25
Corporation Act 58

Declaration of Indulgence 30, 34

Dent, Arthur 10, 48
Doe, Charles, *The Struggler* 80–1
Dryden, John 56

Fell, Margaret 65
Fowler, Edward 35

Gifford, John 12, 16
Gordon, General George Charles 88
Greaves, Richard 58, 83

Hill, Christopher 57, 66, 84–5
Hofmeyer, Isabel 86, 88

International John Bunyan Society 83

Johnson, Samuel 81–2

Keeble, N. H. 33, 63
Kettle, Arnold 45, 84
Kiffin, William 65

L'Estrange, Roger 59
Levellers 9
Lindsay, Jack 84
Livingstone, David 87–8
Luther, Martin 13

Millenarianism 9
Milton, John, *Paradise Lost* 55, 59
Moffat, Robert 87

Nonconformists/Nonconformity 21–2, 25, 31, 34, 42, 49, 56, 62, 66, 77, 84

Offor, George 81
Owens, W. R. 34

Ponder, Nathaniel 34
Popish Plot 49, 56
Presdestination 12–14, 25–6

Quakers 19–20, 22, 30–1, 65, 66

Ranters 19–20, 66
Rye House Plot 62, 66

Scriptures 26–9
Sharrock, Roger 54, 83
Sherman, Thomas 61
Southey, Robert 82
St Paul 18, 21

West, Alick 84

www.ingramcontent.com/pod-product-compliance
Lightning Source LLC
Chambersburg PA
CBHW051110030726
47504CB00006B/1879